Counterfeits

three plays

I0153963

Mark Chrisler

BROADWAY PLAY PUBLISHING INC
New York
www.broadwayplaypublishing.com
info@broadwayplaypublishing.com

cover image by Susie Kirkwood
First printing: June 2015
I S B N: 978-0-88145-605-9

Book design: Marie Donovan
Page make-up: Adobe Indesign
Typeface: Palatino
Printed and bound in the U S A

THE ART OF PAINTING

A previous version of THE ART OF PAINTING was commissioned by The Curious Theatre Branch and opened on 2 July 2010 as part of the show Three Story Animal at Center Portion Gallery in Chicago. It was curated by Beau O'Reilly and performed by the author.

The play opened as part of The New York International Fringe Festival, a production of The Present Company, on 11 August 2012 at Jimmy's No. 43 in New York. It was produced by Found Objects Theatre Grp. The cast and creative contributors were:

THE INSTRUCTOR ....Mark Chrisler

Director ....Tim Racine

Technical director .... Hope Wondowsky

(Lights up on a lecture hall. A projector or easel on which various paintings will be displayed. After a moment, a disheveled INSTRUCTOR *enters; he has a pack of cigarettes in his breast pocket. He addresses the audience.)*

INSTRUCTOR: Welcome, everyone, to *The Art of Painting.* I will be your instructor for this session. Before we get started I see that a number of you failed to bring paints and canvases. Good for you. I'm not going to be teaching you to paint anyway.

To the rest of you who did bring in supplies, I'm sorry; and I understand the confusion. But this class is entitled *"The Art of Painting,"* not *"How to Paint".* Don't get me wrong, knowing how to paint is an important part of painting. No doubt there. One of the most important parts, even. But I can't teach that. I lack the control of color and eye for composition. My paintings are, tersely put, awful.

Now, those of you who have heard of me may wonder why—if I can't paint well—why, then, would I attempt to recreate Vermeer's greatest masterpiece? Why did I do it, you ask?

It's a very good question. And if we have time at the end of the class, I'll try to get to it.

But if we're going to stand a chance of covering those things, we've got to get started on the lesson, the majority of which is...verifiable, although I hesitate to call it true.

Even then, it contains a number of things we must term
'lies,' some perpetrated by myself, others by the people
who lived them and still others by a nameless force
we're going to have to call history.
If you'd like to keep track of the true things and the
not true things, you're welcome to make the effort. If
not, that's fine too. There's still some debate, after all,
about whether the difference is important to *The Art
of Painting*. My father, for instance, believed…well, it
doesn't matter. Every son murders his father, after all.
*(He withdraws a cigarette absentmindedly, then replaces it
before lighting as if correcting a mistake.)*
The Art of Painting. If those of you with paints would
like to attempt to copy it, be my guest. I did, so why
not you. *The Art of Painting*. By Johannes Vermeer,
why not say. And while we're at it—saying things
like that—let's say it's an immensely clever painting.
A masterpiece, even. Ahead of its time. Vermeer
would like that, provided we say it was painted by
him. Which is what we're currently saying. Let's say
the year is 1675, which—let's be frank about it—is
a downright slander, but it's what we're saying.
Vermeer's short period of fame and prosperity is at its
end. In a few hours he will be dead, leaving monstrous
debts for his widow and children. He tried to mitigate
that debt, selling off everyone of his paintings at
whatever price he could get. Except *The Art of Painting*.
That one he kept. Went out of his way to keep. And
it will be the only thing with him when he dies. His
paintings were like his children, and *The Art of Painting*
his favorite son. Vermeer never wanted kids, he only
loved to paint. That said, he also considered fucking a
fun use of his free time, and so he had fourteen kids on
record. Historians speculate he was secretly Catholic.
We'll say the woman, looking freshly shagged, is Clio,
muse of history. We can be pretty confident of that. The

divisions on the map point to a few possible instances
of national incivility in Dutch history. And then there's
the painter: our main interest. A painting of a painter
painting calls to mind the concept of infinite regress; a
process that creates itself over and over forever. Being
a product of 17th century art, we'll have to chalk this
up to coincidence, or us bringing significance from
the future into the randomness of the past. Every son
murders his father.

Let's say it's 1947, which is far less a lie than saying it's
1675, provided we're subscribing to that sort of view
of time. However, we are not; so let's say it's 1947 and
admit to ourselves it's as much a bullshit thing to say
as the last one was. Jacques is fleeing from his last visit
to his father's cell. Han Von Meegeren had been too
holy with him, too oracular, too Grecian. And in a few
hours he'll be dead. He'd always wanted babies. Then
he'd actually had them. He considered his offspring
and his work equally his children, and equally
fraudulent. The former side of this metaphor, the
romantic side, was obvious and alluring. But the latter,
the counter, the monkey-paw irony of this outlook
had surprised him. He remembered the fear he felt
on those Sundays Jacques had refused to attend mass
with him. How his son's absence might expose for the
parishioners a secret amorality pumping through him.
If Jacques went out on the streets grimy or mismatched
wouldn't the neighbors catch wind of the horrid
disorder his father battled daily to contain beneath
a constantly thinning veneer of conviviality and
fastidiousness? What would it say about Han if his son
ended up depressive or queer? What would it mean if
he ended up a cheat or a counterfeiter? Well, of course,
we know what that would mean. It was the same
with the art of painting: every new piece brought into
the world only served to increase the odds of being

exposed. Van Meegeren had held for his whole life that
pictures were just pictures, with no cords to connect
them to their authors. But now, with his lies coming
undone, he feels those cords quite concretely pulling,
slowly splaying his every molecule apart. It's suddenly
reasonable to imagine his children, both the paintings
and his son, going on unblemished into forever, but
disavowing his influence completely. Creation seems
silly and unnecessary to the created. All the things his
father had once said about him must, he now realizes,
in part inform who he is. And looking forward, is there
anyway Jacques won't come one day to agree with his
grandfather on every word of it? Every son murders
his father.

But for Vermeer, his father wasn't really the best
candidate. He was a cloth maker of sorts, with a
moderate interest in art surpassed only by a generous
interest in drinking. His favorite variety—or the one
with which he'd wanted most to better acquaint
himself, at least—was that deep, powerless sort of
black-out drinking that directly precipitated acts of
wanton and unreasonable violence. One night, when
Vermeer was still young, his father saw a grand
opportunity to expand his experience in this perhaps
over-specific area of interest. He was in his bedroom
with Vermeer's mother and the very strong intention
of doing some love-making. Love-making with the
wife. Yessir. For real this time. The last four nights and,
sporadically, several years, had been a series of flukes
attributable, perhaps, to one secretive conspiratorial
agency or another. But not tonight. Tonight the Free
Masons or Illuminati or whoever-the-hell had better
cower, he thought, because I'm feeling—Jesus—I'm
feeling horny and I'm going to give it to the—
fucking hell—I'm going to give it to the old girl, by
God! He stood at the foot of the bed, dressing gown

hiked, rocking back and forth in a way very closely resembling a child making his first attempt at a diving board. Vermeer's mother lay in the dark for minutes, wondering if there were a word for "disinterested anticipation" until, finally, out of the void an eerily convivial "not tonight, love; taking a walk," ushered forth. On the street, full of mumbling anger, he made a straight shot for the pub. He was now, at the least, with the perfect foundation to build that destructive kind of drunkenness.

"Every cloud," and all that. Later that night, right plastered, he beat a random stranger into a coma. Twenty-nine days later the man died and, the same day, Vermeer's father began acquiring art. The intermingling of destruction and rebirth, cliché and didacticism; every son murders his father. Later he bought the pub in which he'd killed, managing it successfully through retirement.

The Art of Painting. In the style of Johannes Vermeer, let's say. Although, honestly, we could just as easily say "in the style of Pieter de Hooch". "Yet, what's important isn't what we could say, but rather what we are saying. And what we are saying is "in the style of Johannes Vermeer," which, as it happens, is every bit as easy. Back in 1675, very intimate now with the feelings of death, Vermeer is staring at *The Art of Painting*. That he has the painting there with him at his end would be great confirmation it was in fact his work, if you had any reason to believe I was relating that sequence correctly, which, as it happens, you do not. Musn't dwell. Back in 1675, very intimate now with the feelings of death, Vermeer is staring at *The Art of Painting*. A canvas which, it doesn't seem that long ago, he had sat at and—with a thought—wavered. It had been a long day. There had been the morning painting, and the mid-day fucking, yes; but before that

the argument. So often the argument. "Look," he'd
told his wife, "I give you money and all I ask is that
you go and spend it". He would often tell his wife
he needed her away while he painted—the creaking
in the floorboards and the so forth—and she had the
only partly mitigated gall to be hurt by this request,
which Vermeer found deeply unfair. But that morning
she'd pointed out a pattern—she called it—that he
only needed her gone—and he said not only, but on
with it—she said he seemed only to need her gone
when he had women in the studio. The implication
was insulting. It wasn't that she was wrong per say,
he certainly did find it easier to paint women after
fucking them, and he certainly did find it difficult to
devote himself wholly—what other way was there—
to fucking strange models with his wife about. Of
course he did; he was, after all, a good and decent
man given to pangs of guilt and self-consciousness
when forced—that was the word for it—when forced
to perform his infidelities in close proximity to his
spouse. But beyond that, he had always felt there was a
deeper, more spiritual reason, more important than the
carnal one, for needing her away, and she'd put him
in the position of having to admit to himself he had
no clue whatsoever what that would be. He wavered,
and it might have been that or the morning painting
with whatever-the-hell-her-name-was; the morning
painting that just felt workmanlike and off until, with
a groaning he fell—crest and all—across his paints
and screamed "where has the rouge gone from your
cheeks?!"

"What?" the model searched.
"Your pallor, miss. You look grave. Seriously grave…
Gravely grave. Like the fatted calf you were has been
blood-let right in front of me. "
"Perhaps the calf just needs a tanning", she suggested.

And then the fucking. It helped with the painting, see.
Painting and fucking: his wheelhouse, he thought.
His wheelhouse and...adjoining wheelhouse. Tandem
wheelhouses. He'd never really worked out the
expression. "I'm going to call you Clio," he'd told the
now damp and Rosy young woman.
"Can't you remember my name?" Vermeer huffed.
That wasn't why at all. Sure, he couldn't remember her
name at the moment—he was sure it would come back
to him—but what a rude presumption. Half-truths, he
thought, were much greater falsehoods than fictions.
"Who's Clio? A schoolyard tart you'd like a nostalgic
go at?" "She's the muse of history. "

The Art of Painting.

The unlit chandelier; if we can analyze a bit—
speculate, really—perhaps symbolizes the Dutch
subjugation of Catholicism. So the painter is probably
a Catholic. But there are more interesting conclusions
we can draw than that. What is the art of painting,
according to the artist of this piece? Painting history.
The muse of history, in this case. Clio.

More interesting, she's not watching over a battle or
accounting the birth of a great king: she's lazing about
as though recovering from a kinetic boinking. And
who's this painting her? These days, with the piece
widely accepted as a Vermeer, there are three popular
theories—two of which are interesting. The third is that
it's merely a stand-in for the idea of an artist. Perfectly
valid hypothesis and totally fucking boring. So we'll
chuck it with prejudice.

The other two well-regarded possibilities are that it is a
self-portrait, Vermeer himself; or his idol, Rembrandt.
Both ideas gained prominence in the early twentieth
century, when the prevailing aesthetic philosophy
said it didn't matter who painted a piece or why.

Only its craft and beauty mattered. This notion, called "significant form" by critic and philosopher Clive Bell, held that a museum could even display, hypothetically, a print or forgery without qualm or hesitation.

It all sounded very good, hypothetically.

Now, some interactive learning: let's say it's 1940. I know, I know.

But let's say it's 1940 and you're a Nazi.

Yeah. Weren't expecting that, were you? You're a big fan of Dutch golden-age painters—because of an idiosyncratic misinterpretation of Nietzsche or Wagner or something else as outwardly incongruous—and you happen to be in Holland for…unrelated reasons. There you find a man, drenched in nicotine and misery, willing to sell you two Vermeers you've never seen before and are eager to get your big, black-leather-gloved, stereotypically S S hands on. But as your men are collecting them, you see a third: *The Art of Painting.* You must have it, you say, for The Fuhrer— not knowing one of your comrades has just procured the same exact painting for the same exact Fuhrer in Brussels. Suddenly reticent and nervous, the man lets off a stink cloud of stale tobacco, carried by his sweaty skin. It takes a considerable effort to convince him to part with the canvas, and more effort still on the part of your men to restrain you from beating him into a coma. When finally it is yours, you look upon it and, with a flourish, address your men: "Do you know what this is? Vermeer's masterpiece: *The Art of Painting.* 'That woman there: she's Clio, the muse of history. You can tell by the horn and the book. Look at her face: almost looks like she's just gotten the bone. Like the painter fucked history. And the painter. You know who that is? It's Rembrandt. Vermeer was obsessed with him. "

"That's a common mistake," blurts the dealer,
suddenly showing way too much spine for a
Dutchmen, "it's a self-portrait, the painter is Vermeer".

"And who do you think you are?" you ask.

"I'm Han van Meegeren and I happen to know
Vermeer's work better than just about anyone."

"Well that's very nice," you say, "but I'm [whatever-
the-hell-your-name-is] and I happen to shoot people
sometimes with little provocation".

And that settled that. For the time being.

Ten Vermeers, including two *Arts of Painting* somehow,
ended up in Nazi hands during the war. Eight would
eventually be found in a mountain cave, one with
Herrmann Goering and one would burn in a bunker
with Adolf Hitler, although it's difficult to say which
one.

And in 1947 an increasingly decrepit Han van
Meegeren would suffer a heart attack and die in jail
before he could be sentenced on charges originally
stemming from treasons through sale of cultural
artifacts to the enemy.

The "dying prematurely of cardiac arrest" strategy was
only one half of a very novel defense on his part.

Let's say Van Meegeren had started out as a painter,
which is almost mostly true. Van Meegeren had indeed
wanted to paint since he first saw the bright colors
and beautiful figures of Vermeer. But painting was
considered by his father a decadent and amoral pursuit
that flew in the faces both of pragmatism and Christian
humility.

It was also, he declared, "a little faggy".

Van Meegeren's first experience with Vermeer was
also his earliest memory. There'd been a pedophile and

serial murderer stalking the streets of Amsterdam for the flesh of errant children, which had reminded the young van Meegeren's father that the boy was overdue to learn some independence.

He dressed his son in his finest, most innocent pantsuit, handed him a sack lunch of what he assumed were edible flower pedals and took him out to the busy streets. After an exhaustibly serpentine walk to an unrecognizable neighborhood, Hans' father offered him some advice: "I'm going to leave you. Just close your eyes and I'll be gone. You've got to make it on your own, but if you get lost or scared, just ask a friendly man to take care of you. Lots of friendly men in the city. Tell them you're alone and naïve and trusting and that if something were to happen to you, no one would even know it. Alright?

(He crosses downstage and kneels.)

"And remember, Han," he said, kneeling to look in his son's eyes, "you're a cheat and you always will be".

Every son murders his father, but that doesn't mean they can't live up to expectations.

There's only one way we could say *Carel Fabritius* lived up to expectations, and it's a bit of a stretch. Almost more a transitionary sentence from one section of a lesson plan to another than an organic observation.

Fabritius was the greatest pupil of Rembrandt, destined to surpass him, and his story will not occupy us long. He was never the painter Rembrandt was, having neither the control of color nor eye for composition needed to be a true master.

Maybe we should amend things and say "every son tries to murder his father."

The only reasonable sense in which Fabritius topped Rembrandt is in that he produced a far greater apprentice than he had ever managed to be. Because Fabritius mentored Vermeer.

Besting his teacher was nothing more than a road apple for Vermeer: it was Rembrandt he had his eye on. There had, so far as he was concerned, never been any better. Rembrandt gave Vermeer moments of true ecstasy and love, made him weep openly and laugh aloud. We could say it was Vermeer's murderous drunk of a father who pushed him towards painting during his brief interest. We could say it was Fabritius who gave him the tools of the trade. But there's no two ways about it: it was Rembrandt that drove him to be great. And Vermeer hated him for it.

Every son murders his father. It was Freud who said so, nearly two hundred years after Vermeer's death. But if he'd heard it, he would have said "I wish I had the fucking chance".

Rembrandt's father—artistically speaking—had been the painter who trained him, *Jacob van Swanenberg*, who you've probably never heard of because of how completely Rembrandt managed to eclipse him.

(He withdraws another cigarette.)

I don't think we even have to say it… Sorry. I suppose there's no smoking here anyway.

(He replaces the cigarette.)

Rembrandt painted with an intense frivolity. Masterful compositions and brilliantly subtle statements came to him at such a furious pace that he would often simply abandon sketches; or paint over paintings. He produced hundreds of pieces, and even those clearly reckless or flawed Vermeer adored.

Yet he allowed himself no such latitude: meticulous and cautious almost to the point of farce. He produced so little work that only at his most popular moments

could he even make a living from it. By the turn of
the 19th century, Vermeer was virtually unknown,
with even his masterpiece *The Art of Painting* being
attributed to his rival, Pieter de Hooch. One hundred
years later, in the early 1900s, interest in Vermeer
sparked, but only thirty odd paintings were known
to exist. That number spiked way above fifty in the
thirties and forties, then crashed violently back down
to thirty-three in 1947.

If you know why, keep it to yourself: I'm trying to play
a kind of a cup game here.

Vermeer would destroy paintings if he felt them going
south even a little bit. It was like covering up a crime: a
feeling any imperfect detail would be evidence he was
a cheat.

So far as we know, Rembrandt destroyed but one
piece: *The Conspiracy of Claudius Civilus*. His magnum
opus. The body politick that had commissioned
it found his statement too strong, too visceral, too
rebellious. Where Vermeer hid away his destructions,
Rembrandt reveled in his: angry and obtuse. Only one
of seven panels survived his rage, the last thing he ever
produced. Vermeer found these events a tragedy for
which there was no contemporary analogue.

If it had been 1947, he'd have called it a holocaust.

Hermann Goering, second in Hitler's command, head
of the Luftwaffe, loved *Christ with The Adulterous*, the
Vermeer acquired for him from van Meegeren. Loved
it like he loved the marauding, fiery destruction of
British civilian structures. Which was to say, a lot. He
displayed it in the main dining room of his main villa,
being sure to point it out to all of his visitors several
times a day. When alone he would stand before it in
reverence and appreciation for hours.

When the war started to turn bad (read: good) he arranged a special convoy of his most decorated guard to spirit it away to an abandoned salt mine, safe from the ravages of allied revenge.

Over the course of the engagement Germany procured thousands of paintings from all the world's great masters. After their surrender, a great effort was undertaken to retrieve Europe's art, track it back through its original dealers and owners, determine their complicity in the theft and either return the work to them or charge them with treason.

This task was generally not as complicated as it sounds because, say what you will about Nazis, they knew how to keep a paper trail. So it usually went something like this:

Knock knock.

"Hello, we found this de Hooch of yours in a Nazi estate. Why'd you give it to them?"

"They were going to kill me. "

"Fair enough! Here you go!"

Or

"Because I hate Jews. I mean…"

"No, no. You already said it. Come with us. "

But things got more complicated when they came to the door of Han van Meegeren. The art dealer was unwilling or unable to explain where he'd gotten Goering's Vermeer, and fairly obstinate about it in his own nervous, chain-smoking, Dutch way.

So he was thrown in jail to await trial for treason. He stayed there six weeks before confessing. Not to selling Dutch culture to the enemy, though. Rather, he confessed to an unprecedented career of forgery, fraud and bilking museums and collectors out of hundreds of millions of guilders.

When Goering was told his Vermeer was a fake...

Hold on, let's start that sentence again. Listen closely:

When Hermann Goering, second in Hitler's command, head of The Luftwaffe was told his Vermeer was a fake, it was said, and I quote, "he looked as though, for the first time he realized there was evil in the world".

Months later he was brought before a firing squad for his part in the systematic murder of six point five million Jews and Gypsies and a failed attempt to take over the motherfucking world.

Among the many things the court, reporters and friends had to ask van Meegeren, perhaps the least answerable was "why did you do it?" He thought about it a lot and always came back to a sagging bed in 1932 where he had quietly wept in the dark.

This was a common occurrence when he tried to have sex with Johanna, his wife. Common, but—he was quick to note—not universal. When his tears interrupted their romance he would gasp out the words plaintively between sobs: "it doesn't happen every time."

Alternatively, when successful he accompanied the moment of orgasm with a jerking yet triumphant "see: no crying this time!" which, as far as Johanna was concerned, was all the worse.

But she understood, even though she didn't. Because van Meegeren either wouldn't or couldn't explain. All it took was a fraction of a second—to lose focus even that long was to invite a tidal wave into his mind: long-gone affairs riddled with regret, half-remembered abuses.

He remembered the game he used to play with his father, where he would attempt to write the phrase "I know nothing, I am nothing, I am capable of nothing" one hundred times before daddy's lashing belt caused him to pass out.

He very rarely won.

He'd defied his father in his teens, telling him he wanted to be an artist. His father had said he'd be an architect, never an artist. Van Meegeren had pointed out that architecture was technically art too, to which his father had retorted "Go fuck yourself, you no talent gypsy."

And that settled that. For the moment.

He thought about that day his father had put him to the streets. The man he found who had not only taken him home, but given him one: The Dutch Museum. The old man led young Han past decadent Picassos and careless Kandinskys. Through room after room of near-sighted French laudanum addicts and into a bright one that felt a refuge, a sanctuary from the horrors of the modern. Here were the Vermeers: colorful, exuberant, pulsing with light. A breeze seemed to blow out from them and directly into the boy's lungs, filling him with both coolness and warmth, excitement and peace.

(He crosses downstage and kneels.)

The old man leaned down then and in his ear whispered "this is as good as it will ever get," and van Meegeren loved Vermeer right then, but hated him too: because he knew the man was right.

Van Meegeren felt the old, craggy lips of that man reach out to his cheek—a kiss that clicked like a turnstile, a moment that waved all past moments away.

Crying in the dark, thinking all those thoughts, van Meegeren hesitated. He could see there the glow of a new off-white canvas, smug in its blankness.

The man had eventually helped him home. The cruelty of it: showing a boy a world replete with color, beauty and majesty only to suck him right out the airlock, back into the grey-brown muck of his larger life, the implacable flagellations of his father's coldness.

But it wasn't the end of their time together. Several times that year—and more frequently in those subsequent—the old man would appear to spirit van Meegeren away from the humdrum. Unannounced, unfurling like a Proustian rope from heaven, or a rock-throwing courter nicking the window of a ripe adolescent who even then and even always was listening just for that.

The two of them would go, sometimes to see the Vermeers, occasionally the Fabritiuses or de Hooches. Other times the man would take van Meegeren by the hand over the rough landing of a torn up building on the outskirts he called his studio. It was here the man did his own painting in the old style. He didn't have the control of color nor eye for composition to keep up with even the second-rate 17th century artists, let alone Vermeer, but he did have a lot of knowhow.

Sort of the artistic equivalent of Socrates' hated sophists: he could stretch a canvas, pestle pigments, mimic the old strokes. And that's what he taught van Meegeren: technique, the old way of doing things. And obsession. Gripping obsession. Rumination, chain-smoking, binge-drinking, stress and self-loathing.

The old man made van Meegeren the greatest 17th century painter in all the 1900s, and that, consequently, made him one of the most miserable men in history.

At twenty he looked thirty, at twenty-five, forty. He hated the world and he hated himself. Sometimes one more than the other but just as often the opposite. Semantics, really.

The only thing left for him to love—once the old man passed on, obscure and usurped, was Vermeer; and he hated him most of anyone.

(He withdraws a cigarette.)

Every son murders his father.

(He pauses, replaces the cigarette.)

I'm trying to quit anyway.

He made a meager living selling his masterpieces for a pittance to tourists and dentists offices while talentless abstract fuckwads chided his lack of originality from million dollar urinals.

In his late thirties, looking in his mid-fifties, the reviews began to really take their toll on him. Every unkind word brought out memories of his father: trodden, stale, Paleolithic; cheat, talentless, gypsy. They made him feel his father's every word had been true. Well, not the gypsy part. Van Meegeren thought that was a stretch.

Worse still was the faint praise: that he'd have been a great Vermeer if only there hadn't already been one two hundred years before. And then, staring through the night at that big blank canvas pulsing towards him, breathing, van Meegeren came upon what seemed the most obvious idea of his life. If his paintings would have made great Vermeers, he'd just has to pass off one of his paintings as a Vermeer, wouldn't he?

For the next five years he worked on the perfect forgery, culminating in the creation of a new Vermeer masterpiece he hoped to sell to a museum before revealing that it was he who had painted it, thereby forcing the art world to respect him.

It was a plan that would end up working too well. But at first he focused on studies—composed by memory—of Vermeer's great progeny. He first heard Freud's statement "every son murders his father" from his wife while creating his first study on the large canvas.

"It's funny you should mention it," he said, and returned to work on a counterfeit *Art of Painting* that would eventually wind up—quite unknown and accidentally—in Nazi hands.

Art of Painting was Vermeer's largest canvas, and arguably his most symbolic painting, as he didn't much go in for that sort of thing. The figure in the painting, looking freshly fucked, would be Clio, the muse of history. The unlit chandelier would represent The Dutch subjugation of Catholicism. The divided map, either the fall of The Great Dutch Empire Rembrandt witnessed or the occupation of Flanders in Vermeer's time.

It's difficult to say which because it's difficult to determine who the painter represents: Rembrandt or Vermeer.

It does, at first glance, resemble portraits of *Rembrandt:* black garb and large red hair. Unfortunately, the best image we have to represent Vermeer is his painting The Procuress which shows him dressed, lit and posed—no kidding—as Rembrandt in this famous self-portrait, except that he is lecherously participating in the sexual assault of a waitress.

One more time: the only self-portrait we have of Vermeer shows him as Rembrandt during the overture to a probable gang rape. Seriously. Take a look.

(The Procuress)

Every son murders his father. And that, you'll excuse my saying so, is, like, the second most creative way to get it out of your system I can think of.

Six hours after banging what's-her-face (he'd decided to just go with Clio) Vermeer was feeling pretty pleased with himself, which he knew to be a dangerous thing. "Pleased with himself" was exactly how he usually felt right before he ruined something irreparably.

Still, the piece was really coming along at a healthy clip, and he couldn't help but feel he was on to something. No, not just on to something, he thought: fucking on to something.

Here he was, capturing the very nature of art, he figured. Painting a painter recreating history at her most beautiful. Post-coital.

Marking their place, that was it. Even Rembrandt had never revealed the essence of his own duty. This, then would be the piece that exceeded him, succeeded him. Every son murders his father. And suddenly, Vermeer felt sad.

In that moment, before the canvas, he hesitated. The might-as-well-be Clio had left her pose and came around behind to look at him working. He hated when they did that.

"That me?" she asked.

"Clio."

"Right. Clio. And is that you painting me? Her?"

"No," he said and then paused very dramatically in a rhetorical flourish to coda with profundity his revelation. "No, that's my father."

(Pause)

"The drunken man-slaughterer?" she asked, ruining everything.

"No. The other one."

Vermeer painting Rembrandt, van Meegeren painting Vermeer, me painting van Meegeren. Patricide upon patricide. Infinite regress.

Did Johannes Vermeer see any significance to it all, staring at *The Art of Painting* in the moments before losing consciousness for the last time, back in 1675? Probably he just muttered to himself that Rembrandt would never have died like him: broke, alone, reviled, leaving his family in debt. Of course, this was precisely how Rembrandt had died, and Vermeer knew it. But dying gives bitterness an odd tannin. Perhaps Vermeer died dreaming of posthumous discovery and appreciation. Even in 1675 the cliché of the artist made rich and famous only after his death was common. It had started with Rembrandt. The shithead.

Van Meegeren, conversely, had fame and fortune at his death—although if there was comfort to be taken from that, he'd missed the instructions. His first phony Vermeer, *Supper at Emmaus*, had been swallowed hook, line and sinker, but when it landed in a major museum, van Meegeren did not come forward to claim it and shame the art world. Instead he took the seven million guilders it was purchased for and began working on a second…then a third. Soon he was rich beyond his ability to spend. He purchased houses, villas, cars and art, including—with no small irony—several minor Vermeers. Most say that, whatever started him out, van Meegeren's forging became about the cash. But he quite literally continued producing and selling past the point where he had any idea what to do with the gains. To this day people occasionally find boxes stuffed with hundreds of thousands of guilders, buried awkwardly and desperately; like the result of an incredibly expensive episode of *I Love Lucy*. Incredibly expensive and, let's level, probably pretty hilarious.

It was, let's say, a compulsion. An addiction. A compulsion to paint and an addiction to seeing the paintings pass. A compuldiction, an addipulsion. He had never really worked out the expression. Even though every new piece put his lie at risk, he continued working. Even though he faced the possibility of a firing squad, he went six weeks before coming clean. For his son, he'd say. By which, I'll tell you, he meant himself.

When he did admit to forging the many Vermeer's he'd brokered, no one believed him. The prosecution brought in expert witness after expert witness: collectors who had purchased the fakes, curators who'd displayed them, critics who'd lauded them. All agreed van Meegeren was lying about lying about the paintings. At some point the court asked him if he could prove his case by creating a new forgery. Han said he could, if provided with the right supplies. And so for the next four days, van Meegeren went to work before the court, with the help of his hand-mixed paints, hand-stretched canvas, hand-smoked carton of cigarettes and hand-guzzled gallon of bourbon. His wife and son were in attendance, and Jacques learned a lot about the old ways. He ended up with *Jesus Among The Doctors*, definitive proof of his relative innocence and the last van Meegeren forgery. For the time being.

The Dutch people fell in love with the man who'd defrauded Goering. He polled the second most popular figure in Holland, just behind the Dutch prime minister. But the fame comforted his final moments as little as the fortune. Convicted of fraud, he died awaiting sentencing in jail shortly after attempting to salvage some legacy with his son, Jacques. Han had hated and defied his dad, loved and usurped his mentor, rued and damaged his hero. Above everything, he didn't want the trend to continue with his son.

He'd told him "I have to leave you now. You have to make it on your own, but if you get lost or scared, just know that I'm always watching you.

(He crosses downstage and kneels.)

"And remember, Jacques," he said, kneeling down to look in his eyes, "you're my son and you always will be.

And then the running. Jacques had recoiled from that charge as from a wicked curse, a frost giant's glyph emblazoning his forehead. It broke Han's heart.

Not literally. I don't mean literally. What literally broke his heart was a lifetime of alcoholism, chain-smoking and type-A personality stress strategies. And, of course, genetics. From the father's side.

The closest thing we have to a cause of death for Vermeer is a letter his wife wrote, stating "as a result and owing to the very great burden of his children, having no means of his own, he had lapsed into such a decay and decadence, which he had so taken to heart that, as if he had fallen into a frenzy, in a day or day and a half he had gone from being healthy to being dead." Van Meegeren's said of him only "he couldn't survive in so bright a shadow". Although, once again, I'm prone to believe the medical examiner's less romantic explanation of "heart attack".

Van Meegeren had not given a full accounting of his fakes before his death, and that, let's say, caused some problems. Some Vermeers have a clear enough provenance that we can be sure of them.

The Girl with The Pearl Earring, real.

Some were exposed by van Meegeren at trial.

Woman Drinking, fake.

But others lack either kind of concreteness, and some have as much doubt as support. Or more. *Smiling Girl,* we can't say. This uncertainty resulted in a steep decline in the value of Vermeer paintings, as well as several other Dutch painters van Meegeren had forged. *The Music Lesson,* let's say…real.

On the other hand, van Meegeren was now such a figure—a curiosity to some, a folk hero to others—that his paintings, once practically worthless, rocketed in value. Even the forgeries.

Interior with Drinkers, let's say fake.

Harder hit still than Vermeer's reputation was that of the philosophers and museums who had held nothing mattered save the beauty of the painting. Suddenly the subjunctives were real and people felt there was an actual value—not just money, but to their appreciation—that came from being in the presence of a true masterpiece.

Christ in The House of Martha and Mary, probably real.

Even most of those who considered van Meegeren's products paintings and not just forgeries couldn't help but feel his story was important to their quality.

Lady Reading Music, fake, depending on what you mean.

Museums that had said the originality or authorship of a piece of work was unimportant no longer said this, or at least—if they did—said it quietly. No curator would knowingly hang a van Meegeren. Where would it go? Putting it with the Dutch Renaissance would be disingenuous, lumping it with the moderns incongruous.

If, however, you happened to be a museum with
the luck—and we'll use the word loosely—to have a
questionable Vermeer in your gallery, like, say *Boy
with a Little Dog*, the math is pretty easy. X-ray and
radioscopic dating could confirm the provenance, but
why bother? As it stands it might be worth, say, eight
million dollars. Prove it's a Vermeer once and for all
and you might add three to that. Find out it's a fake
and you can expect it to sell for forty grand on a good
day, and you're not going to hang it in your darkest
closet. And so, many pieces like *The Rommel Pot Player*
continue to decorate major museums.

The Art of Painting: The last great masterpiece of the
tortured Vermeer. Or the first grand study of the
haunted van Meegeren. Which hated hero does the
artist represent: Rembrandt or Vermeer? The potential
loss from the answer is orders of magnitude greater
than *Boy with a Little Dog*, so it's not unreasonable
to say we'll never know. It leaves this painting the
conclusion of two stories in superimposition, bound
to drift together, bound both to inhabit and inhibit
one another. Maybe just as van Meegeren would
want. And in that same sense, perhaps Vermeer
would appreciate being inseparably confused with
Rembrandt. All of which begins to look almost like
an ending, if you squint hard and at the right angle.
But the painter paints the painter painting the painter
painting the painter…etc.

It only took fifteen years for the ground to shift under
van Meegeren's reputation. New van Meegeren
forgeries were popping up and, much to everyone's
surprised, they all shared a common attribute: *they
were awful*. Even a casual observer wouldn't confuse
them with Vermeers. Was it possible World War Two
had so panicked the art scene that they were blind to
van Meegeren's inability? Or was his true fraud taking

credit for fakes that had been real? Had collectors and museums bargain-basement sold more than a dozen of the more priceless art works in history?

These possibilities tanked van Meegeren's posthumous career. As a skilled forger who'd tricked Nazis he was an icon, but as a third-rate hack who got lucky on a lie, and who just maybe did sell to Goering, there wasn't much to love. And then there was *The Art of Painting*. If the one on display in Austria now had been by van Meegeren, it should have been as shitty as the other forgeries. Since it decidedly was not, van Meegeren's must have been the one destroyed with Hitler. And that settled that. For a very brief moment.

Then, another *Art of Painting* was found. That didn't make sense. There should only have been two: Vermeer's and van Meegeren's. One should have been destroyed and the other should have been in a museum. Suddenly there were suspicions about fake fakes. An investigation quickly found a confessor who had taken, it seemed, to forging van Meegeren's forgeries of Vermeer. The biggest clue had been within the newly discovered *Art of Painting*: the artist looked neither like Rembrandt or Vermeer, but like a sweaty, broken, miserable, chain-smoking fraud.

Even with interest in the story renewed, his reputation never quite bounced back, the new van Meegerens, the meta-frauds permanently ruined him.

And so, every term, people come to this class—they don't bring paints, they don't bring canvases. They just bring that one question: "Jacques, why did you do it?"

Well, in Dutch we say "Iedere zoon vermoordt zijn vader,"

(He withdraws a cigarette.)

Every son murders his father.

(He lights the cigarette, exits. Blackout)

END OF PLAY

LIST OF PAINTINGS

The Art of Painting, Johannes Vermeer

Fabritius, Self-Portrait, Carel Fabritius 1645

Jacob van Swanenberg, Portrait of a Man in an Oriental Costume, Rembrandt, 1635*

The Conspiracy of Claudius Civilus, Rembrandt

Christ with The Adulterous, Han van Meegren, in the style of Vermeer

Pictures of Rembrandt Self Portrait, Rembrandt, 1629

"Take a look" *The Procuress,* Johannes Vermeer

Supper at Emmaus, Han van Meegeren, in the style of Vermeer

Jesus Among The Doctors, Han van Meegeren, in the style of Vermeer

Girl with a Pearl Earring, Johannes Vermeer

Woman Drinking, Han van Meegeren, in the style of Frans Hals

Smiling Girl, Johannes Vermeer (possibly Han van Meegeren)

The Music Lesson, Johannes Vermeer, 1662-65

Interior with Drinkers, Han van Meegeren, in the style of Pieter de Hooch

Christ in The House of Martha and Mary, Vermeer, 1655

Lady Reading Music, van Meegeren

Boy with a Little Dog, Frans Hals (possibly van Meegeren)

The Rommel Pot Player, Frans Hals (possibly van Meegeren)

"They were awful" Montage of pieces by Jacques van Meegeren**

*Note: this is not actually a portrait of van Swanenberg or by him. This is a deliberate lie.

**In the original production, one canvas with four of Jacques van Meegren's paintings on it were used, but multiple images or, even just one, could suffice. Or another lie would do well here; a fake Jacques van Meegren of a fake Han van Meegren of a fake Vermeer, perhaps.

1 Italicized text indicates when the slide should be advanced to the painting of that title.

PHONIES, FRAUDS AND FAKES

(A Play That is Absolutely Not About my Ex-Girlfriend)

PHONIES, FRAUDS AND FAKES was first staged as part of Curious Theatre Branch's Rhinoceros Theatre Festival. It was produced by Found Objects Theatre Group and opened at Chicago's Prop Thtr on 18 January 2014.

MARK..Mark Chrisler

Lighting...Stefan Brün

(MARK *take the stage: He sits at a table, on which is a small easel that holds a variety of illustrations, next to him is a larger easel upon which is a large poster reading "The Greatest Lie Ever Told". As he begins the first story, he produces a variety of low-rent puppets to illustrate it: a knock-off Barbie doll for Bertrande, a club-carrying caveman for Pierre, two identical action figures for the two Martin's, one with a leg removed, etc.)*

MARK: In 1548, Martin Guerre of Toulouse, France was accused of stealing grain from his father. Martin's first response to the charge was to declare his innocence. His second response, however, was to flee the country to parts unknown for a period of eight years, which, for some people, might slightly undercut that claim.

Casting more doubt still, Martin returned in 1556 to his wife and child, waiting—it appeared—until his father had passed on and, thus, all grain-thieving charges rendered moot. Martin was apologetic about his nearly decade-long absence, but not so apologetic as to explain where the hell he'd been. Still, his wife took him back with seemingly little hesitation, by the historical account.

He went on to sire three more children with her, before finally summoning up the gall to ask for his inheritance. Unfortunately for Martin Guerre, though, his share of his father's largess had already been snapped up by one Pierre Guerre, Martin's paternal uncle who had married his wife's widowed mother while Martin was away, as that sort of creepy, pseudo-incest was yawned at in the era.

So Martin sued his uncle-cum-father-in-law for his share, at which point Pierre decided that Martin was an impostor. Pierre found a wandering soldier with a drinking problem who claimed to have known Martin during the period of his absence. The alcoholic infantryman said Martin had fought with him in the war, and that the last time he had seen him, Martin had just had his leg amputated after suffering a wound from a cannon.

Now armed with the soldier's testimony, Pierre took the next step towards fair and impartial justice: ambushing Martin with a club and beating him for as long as it took for Martin's wife to intervene on his behalf.

A year later, having exhausted the legal recompense a good cudgeling could provide, Pierre sought to file suit against Martin. But Pierre had a problem: only Martin's legal wife could make a formal claim of imposture, and as it happened, she believed, loved and supported Martin. So Pierre dreamed up the sort of clever scheme that only a guy who's first plan of action was "hit him with a table leg" could: he went to the courthouse and forged his daughter-in-law's signature. When the court official asked, he told him that he was not forging the signature, but merely signing for her, because she couldn't make it down to do so herself for reasons he declined to elaborate upon. Even in the sixteenth century, France was a well-respected country based on law and due-process, so, when presented with this outlandish and inexplicable excuse, the court officer said "fair enough! Here you go!" and issued the complaint without hesitation.

By the time the trial came around, Pierre and his wife—whom, again, we must note was both Martin's mother-in-law and aunt—seem to have convinced Martin's wife to support the charge she had not actually filed. She testified that she had believed the man who showed up in 1556 to be her husband, and that she had continued to believe that over the last four years during which she bore him three children, but that in the last few months she'd been convinced he was an impostor. As evidence, she noted that before his absence, he'd been a cold-fish in bed, almost frigid, but that since his return he'd been nearly insatiable, thus the three kids in four years.

Martin, for his end, gave an identical account of their sex lives, not having heard his wife's testimony. When that knowledge didn't convince, Martin turned to an act of romantic histrionics only The French could take as a serious act pursuant of justice. He challenged his wife: he said he would gladly go to the gallows if she would look him in the eyes and swear he was not her husband. She said nothing.

All the same, Martin was convicted and sentenced to death. He immediately appealed to parliament, saying that his money-grubbing uncle was trying to have him besmirched and killed so that he could keep his share of the inheritance. Which, all things being equal, sounded pretty damn likely. So Pierre was arrested for perjury. In the new trial, Martin argued in his own defense, saying that his wife was pressured by his uncle to betray him. He was subjected to an intense and intensive battery of questions regarding his past, all of which he answered accurately and in detail.

The historical record has the jury eating out of Martin's hand during the proceedings, and everyone seems to agree he would have won the case and had Pierre's head on a pike, had a man not appeared in Toulouse mid-trial also claiming to be Martin Guerre. The new man was brought into the court where he proved to have a knowledge of Guerre's past equally as exhaustive as that of the man on trial. What's more, the two were virtually identical. Well, not quite. There was one notable difference in the new alleged Martin's appearance which became noticeable when he rolled up his pants and revealed a wooden peg in place of his missing leg.

And with that, the long-time impostor, whom history knows as Arnaud du Tilh, was sentenced to death for adultery and fraud. He maintained his innocence until all hope of avoiding his execution was exhausted and then, finally, came clean.

Why had he done it? Martin Guerre was not much richer or more respected than Arnaud du Tilh had been, and he only learned of the inheritance well after he had come into the missing man's shoes. The answer Arnaud gave was anticlimactic in the way that so many of the great true stories about great real phonies are: he had been walking around one day, passing through Toulouse, when a man had mistaken him for Martin Guerre. Arnaud corrected the man, at which point he began to tell Arnaud about Guerre, his life, wife and disappearance. Arnaud wished him well and they parted ways. Several hours later, a second man approached him thinking he was Guerre, and this time… Arnaud went with it. He'd been mistaken for Martin twice in one day, and had learned a considerable amount about his life from the first mistaken gent. So Arnaud decided he would pretend to be Martin because…he figured he could probably do it. That was all.

And for that, he was hung in front of the house he had pretended was his on September 16th, 1560, while the

woman he had called his wife and the man he had
called himself watched on.

*(He now directly and flatly addresses the audience, more
conversationally.)*

Is this the greatest lie ever told? Because that's what
we're searching for here tonight. And if you're
thinking "yes, I think that this Arnaud guy is the
greatest liar in history," then *you* must be at a loss for
what we're going to do with the rest of the evening.
Also, if you think I'd open with the best story, I never
want to get a mix-tape from you. Ever. Every good-
thinking mix-tape maker knows that you always open
with your second best song and conclude with the
topper. And if that means that the middle lags a bit,
that's the risk you run. But our safety is that, while we
may have to wait until the end for the best lie, even a
third rate story about a fraud is better than a first rate
story about an honest man.

Like I say, we're here tonight to find the best lie ever
told, and that's a tall task, not least of which because…
how do you qualify something like that? There are so
many potential criteria. Like, the most beautiful lie: a
loving God.

(He unveils a picture of a beautiful, heart-shaped cloud.)

Or, the most impossible lie: a loving God.

*(He replaces the previous picture with that of a mushroom
cloud.)*

There's one that's dead on arrival, too, and it happens
to be the most obvious: the most successful lie.

(He unveils a diagram of toupees.)

But "The Most Successful Lie" has a problem I like to
call The No Good Toupee Fallacy. The goal of a toupee
is to be unobservable, therefore one can never, by
observation, declare that there are no good toupees.

The observed sample set can only include the failures. It may be true that there are no good toupees, but it is a truth that remains forever unverifiable. Say what you will about the complications of string-theory or the mechanics of emergent systems: toupee quality is the foremost area of intellectual concern that can never, ever be sated. And that's also true of successful liars. There could be thousands of liars so successful and amazing that their stories wouldn't be safe to tell around open flames or domestic animals, but we can never, by nature, know those stories. By that standard, the greatest lie ever told could be told by one of you. Or by me.

So that's no good. So, maybe most audacious lie? That might belong to conman Victor Lustig...

(Here, a picture of any gangster-looking man who is NOT Victor Lustig will do.)

...not so much for selling The Eiffel Tower—twice—or for selling a counterfeit-counterfeit money machine, but for running one on the most dangerous man in America, Al Capone. Lustig approached Capone with a business deal: he told Capone that if he would invest fifty thousand dollars with him, he would double it in two months. Capone gave him the money, which Lustig put in a safety deposit box and...went about his day. He just let the money sit there for two months, then he returned to Capone, with an apology, saying that the deal had fallen through and that he was sorry but that he had managed to salvage the original fifty grand. Capone, impressed with Lustig's honesty, gave him a thousand dollars for his trouble and sent him on his way, which was exactly what Lustig had hoped for.

But this is a lie about money. Which, don't get me wrong: money is a fine thing to lie about, one of the old-standbys, but it's a little base and common for consideration as "the greatest lie."

Another possible standard by which to judge a lie might be something like this:

(He unveils a card reading "MY EX-GIRLFRIEND")

Oops. That's not supposed to… Okay, I should probably address this. If you read any of the promotional materials for this show, or the…well, the full title, you might be under some misapprehensions about its contents. Because they seem to point to this show being about my ex-girlfriend, by manner of saying that it's not about my ex-girlfriend. When I first pitched this play, I thought I was going to do this clever little bulshitty meta-play where I would pretend to talk about lies and famous liars and whatever, but there'd be this sort of thin ruse where the performance would go wrong and end up with me just talking about my ex-girlfriend. However, after I turned in the promotional materials for the play I thought I would write, I had to actually, like…write it. And that's where the trouble came in. Because it's not really much of a story. I met this troubled girl, online…and her life was a helluva story, but isn't really relevant to the discussion. She was an orphaned British ex-pat who was suffering from severe lupus that was destroying her liver and…it was just a big fucking mess of a story. And…I didn't meet her for a long time. She was really circumspect about getting together, face to face. And it dragged out for a long while before she finally confessed that the pictures she had represented herself with were…not her. Were someone else. So, I called it off and haven't heard from her since. So, dumb-dumb me. But an almost standard story these days, I think. Or, not standard, but…unexceptional. Not worth building a show around. But I wrote this whole boring shebang about it and got some snide, solipsistic cards

made before backing out and... Anyway, the point
is: while originally this play was supposed to be "not
about my ex-girlfriend" in an ironic, self-defeating,
wink-wink-nudge-nudge kind of way, it has turned
out to be, honestly and truthfully, not about my ex-
girlfriend. So, if for some inexplicable reason you came
here hoping to hear about my ex-girlfriend, first off:
what's wrong with you? And second off: my apologies.
Oh, and third off: there will be no refunds, because
technically the show never advertised itself as being
about my ex-girlfriend anyway. To the contrary.

(He flips to the next page of the script.)

"At this point, you probably gave up on me replying to
this..."

And...that's something else.

(He throws this page away.)

This has already taken a wonderful turn. Jesus. Okay,
um, another criterion we definitely won't use, but that I
will talk about anyway because it is my favorite, is "my
favorite lie."

*(On "The Martian Canals" he reveals a picture of the
canals.)*

*(Several more pictures, of canal maps and then actual Mars
photos, accompany this story.)*

Not much of a contest here: my personal favorite lie
is hands-down The Martian Canals. These were first
"discovered" by Giovanni Schiaparelli in 1877 when
he looked through his telescope at Mars and said "hey!
There are canals all over Mars! Big fuck-off Canals
running pretty much the height of the whole planet!"
And once Giovanni Schiaparelli said this, everybody
who looked up at Mars started agreeing with him. Or
going even further. Some people said that not only
were there canals, but they were straight along the

lines of latitude and obviously made by intelligent beasts. Some people mapped them. People described the effects of The Martian seasons upon them. People wrote books and papers—scientific ones—about how the canals transfer water between oceans and the problems the arid tropics must cause The Martians.

I don't want to spoil anything for you guys here, but—just to be clear—there are zero canals on Mars. And, more disappointingly still, no Martians. Which, okay: they couldn't have said that in 1877—absence of evidence is not evidence of absence, as they say—but as far as the canals go, they are obviously not around. For a while, no one seemed to disagree with the canal theory. People who didn't see them—which is to say, everyone—either kept their mouths shut or pretended they did. And as telescopes got better and skeptics started finding their nerve, the story and observations changed over and over: no, no: we said there used to be water. The canals are dry now. Obviously the Martians are in deep trouble, if they are not already dead. And so we get The War of The Worlds, which ends up turning into a pretty wonderful lie of its own under Orson Welles.

It took pretty well until the 1920s to completely dissolve the canal fraud. How many people had tricked themselves into seeing what they thought they should see? How many had just pretended? How many had lied? And why, oh why, don't we suspect we could be doing the same thing right now?

It's a great story. I fucking love it. But it's also a huge mess. It contorts and transmogrifies every few months, it's needlessly elaborate and…it's inelegant, is what it is. And one thing I feel is probably a very good criterion for our best lie is "elegance," which I mean in the true and scientific definition of the word. A simple thing from which much comes. A great lie should be

profoundly simple, and by its simplicity should expose
some great truth. That's the hope.

But maybe the shortcoming of these stories isn't the
wrong criteria, maybe it's that we're looking at the
wrong species. Human beings may tell the most lies—
after all, we talk the most—but there are plenty of
animal contenders that deserve their shot at the crown.

(Now a photo of an octopus)

The octopus, for example: the greatest marine shyster
of them all. The first, and most fundamental reason
to deceive is to ameliorate predation risk, or, to put
it simply: to keep your ass from getting eaten. And
the octopus is the most accomplished camouflagist in
the animal kingdom, able to alter not only its color,
but also its shape, size and texture in order to avoid
detection. In order to do this, it has the largest brain of
any invertebrate. And that's where the octopus starts
to get really fascinating: brains are very expensive
things. They require lots of energy to run and even
more to build. What makes the octopus' brain size
such an anomaly isn't just that it rests inside a squishy,
weird, spineless creature, but that octopuses—that's
the plural, by the way: people will go back and forth
on "octopi versus octopus." Neither are correct.
Octopuses. It's Greek. Write it down. But the really
strange thing about octopus brains are that octopuses
themselves are incredibly short lived. They don't
tend to make it past three years old. And they're
solitary, meeting only in territory squabbles or, once,
to mate. Big brains are—in every other instance—
reserved to long-lived and social animals: they're too
intensive an investment for short lifespans and not
particularly useful if they're not being deployed in a
communicative setting.

But the kind of camouflage an octopus employs is cognitively intense: computer imaging and analysis have shown that there is no simple or even accurate similarity to be found between a hidden octopus and the things it's disguising itself as. An octopus doesn't look like the stuff it looks like. Instead, it somehow manages to alter its appearance to what you, looking at it, thinks things look like.

I'm having trouble explaining this properly. Here: let's look at a different example: orchids.

In order to copulate, orchids are dependent on insects and birds visiting their flowers and spreading pollen between them. While many flowers lure their pollinators in by being yummy, some orchids use a different and far more insidious method: sexual deception.

(He unveils a bee orchid picture.)

And here's where the difference between true mimicry and deception becomes clear: while we look at this plant and say "hey! It kinda looks like a bee!" the bee looks at it and says "I LOVE YOU!"

Outsiders can make out a resemblance, the bee can make out nothing but. And, apparently, the target creature not only sees one of its own in the orchid, but its perfect match.

(He unveils a picture of a wasp orchid.)

The wasp is known even to ejaculate upon this wasp orchid. It's a perfect lie, not because it is universally undetectable, but because of how fully it fools its target.

Of course, that's only one possible explanation for the orchid's success. Some entomologists argue that an orchid's chosen pollinator—be it bee, wasp, fly or what-have-you—is no more convinced by the flower's

lie than we are. That instead the desirable qualities of
the orchid are built to make the creature ignore the
deception, rather than to believe it. To say, in effect, "I
don't care that she's not real: I still love her."

*(He unveils the fake Ivy picture—a pretty but bookish girl—
unknowingly.)*

Perhaps the appeal of a fiction built specifically for you
supersedes the animal's suspicions and doubts. After
all, does this really look like a butterfly to you?

(He notices the Ivy picture, quickly removes it.)

(A moment)

Okay. So maybe I didn't call it off. I haven't been
entirely forthright with you on that. The truth of the
thing is that, when Ivy—when this girl—revealed her
true appearance, I...she wasn't attractive. Very wasn't
attractive. She had a tremendous amount of weight
around her middle, a slight but noticeable hump on
her back, a remarkably large, round, moon face, some
facial hair, some pocking... And, I think—I must have
felt—that it would be petty or superficial of me to
call off a potentially rewarding relationship because
I wasn't sexually attracted to her. Which, I now
realize, is kinda ridiculous. There are people out there
who no doubt would find Ivy—this girl—attractive,
and pretending that I did—lying—was not an act of
nobility or altruism on my part, it was a small and
secret cruelty of which she was never fully unaware.
She bought that lie, the lie that I found her beautiful,
because it was exactly what she wanted.

So I didn't leave. I told her I understood what had
happened: that she hadn't expected to find a real
relationship through OK-Goddamn-Cupid because
who fucking would? And that the time it took for our
correspondence to develop only made it more and
more impossible to come clean. I told her it was alright,

I understood; I made the excuses for her. She cried,
apologized, told me I was right. She'd been scared of
me leaving, scared that perhaps her "lying problem"
—and that was all she said about that—had returned.
Then I gave her the ultimatum. Well, ultimatum-slash-
amnesty:

"Right here, right now," I told her, "I need you to tell
me if there's anything else, any other lies, because right
now I am understanding and forgiving, but after today
I will not understand, I will not forgive."

She said "no." There was nothing else.

So I stayed. I stayed out of a misguided sense of
magnanimity, or because I still…I don't know why I
stayed.

Her appearance, by the way—hump, trunk-weight,
moon-face—are all symptoms of Cushing's Syndrome;
a condition usually brought about from prolonged
steroid usage. Such as if, you know, you're dying from
lupus. So…bully on me.

(Rejoining the script)

Anyway. Back to it.

There are a few kinds of lies that we presume to be
unique to us humans. And one of those is the kind we
make when we go along with something we know—
on some level—to be false. I'm surprised I don't hear
more people talk about this, because I know that I do it
all the time. Friends, strangers, everybody: sometimes
someone tells you something that you just know is
bullshit. And you know it's bullshit because it's exactly
the sort of bullshit that you say. And so there's a
sort-of wink-wink arrangement made—without any
acknowledgement—that you'll let your girlfriend slide
on saying she's seen *Rashomon* because she believed
you—or seemed to, anyway—when you said you'd

read the latest Lauren Slater novel. If you went calling people on those little fibs left and right, you'd be admitting that you make them, too, and it would make you less trustworthy to the person you exposed than they'd become to you. As far as I know, this is not a theory being floated or tested by the sorts of people that do those things—game theorists and the like—it's just a flight of fancy of mine. But there is some small anecdotal evidence behind it; namely, that a good hoodwink usually relies on finding a dishonest target, someone who spends enough of their time on the defense that they don't have the energy to question the con being pulled on them.

(He turns to the next page. As reading:)

"At this point, you probably gave up on me replying to this. I'm sorry that it took me a while."

(He stops. Turns to the next page, aggravated.)

"I spent a long time thinking about it and working up to it because…"

(MARK stops, more aggravated. He turns to the next page, looks at it. Flips again. And again. And then quickly the scans through the rest of the script: no good. He puts it away. Or throws it)

What was I…oh! The kinds of lies unique to humans. Alright, so, like I said…there's the kind where…where you, you know…fuck…where you go along with lies! And…we talked about that. And then I was going to tell you about…

Um… Yes! The thing about liars—human liars, I mean—is that we're not very good. We're not especially adept at it—or not most of us, at least. It's mentally taxing to lie and, because of that, we all have tells. See, the truth is easy: the truth is accessible. To summon up an honest answer, all we have to do is recall. And recollection is just sitting there, waiting for us to pick it up. Lying, on the other hand, is a building project: a lie has to be created, in the moment, through imaginative effort.

But it has to look easy—like recollection—in order to pass. And so, under the strain of that, lies get conspicuous. We sweat or tremble or go red in the face. We stammer and caveat. And, of course, a lack of confidence or a fear of being caught—or, maybe more desperately, a fear of the very truth we're avoiding—causes us to break eye contact, to look away.

Lucky for liars, we're also extraordinarily bad at detecting lies. We can afford to be so bad at lying precisely because we're equally bad at calling them out. In studies, people show an ability to decipher truth from falsehood that's about as good as a coin flip.

So, it stands to reason, even an impressive lie can be devalued by the gullibility of its target. Inversely, the more suspicious or informed the victim, the more a successful con amazes.

The ultimate, greatest lie possible, then? Self deception.

By definition, self-deception requires the person to know exactly what the truth is—what is being avoided—in order to create a falsehood over it that convinces them to neglect what they, themselves, know.

It's incredible. That kind of thing doesn't come cheap: it's a lot of brainpower, is uniquely human and is definitely, without question, the grandest, biggest, most impressive kind of lie.

A couple decades ago, two psychologists were wondering if there were a way to measure self-deception, and they weren't having a lot of good ideas.

So, out of frustration, they hit the bar one night and started getting properly hammered.

Four or five drinks in, it occurred to them: what if we compiled a list of questions—horrifyingly embarrassing and uncomfortable questions—of things that are probably true of everyone, but that we don't like to admit to ourselves? They agreed this was a very good idea.

Then, they had a few more drinks.

And a couple more.

And then they started writing the self-deception questionnaire that's fascinated researchers ever since.

The questions themselves are great fun: do you enjoy your bowel movements, do you want to fuck every attractive person you see, have you ever fantasized about killing yourself to get back at people—but what makes the questionnaire so amazingly riveting is what we've learned about chronic self-deceivers through it.

Like: the more self-deceptive you are, the better athlete you'll be. Or, the more money you'll make. The longer your relationships will last. The happier you'll be. The longer you'll live.

On every measure of achievement to which the questionnaire has been applied, the liars outstrip the honest by gigantic margins. Save perhaps for attending a good preschool, lying to yourself maybe the single best thing you can do to improve your lot in life. So… why does it feel so icky?

I score very poorly on the test, and I feel really good about that. As much as I champion lying, I'm apparently quite honest with myself. And, even though I know that's a bad thing, I feel proud about it. Weird, huh?

Now, folks: we've gotten somewhere. Maybe you hadn't noticed, but we have. Because we've learned, from these things, some traits, some criteria for our greatest lie: from Al Capone's conman we know a lie should be "confident." Martin Guerre taught us that the liar must be "dedicated." The octopus shows us that a great lie is mostly about "perspective." The orchid...don't worry about the orchid. And, most importantly, from two drunken, shameless psychologists, we must consider the difficulty of the target on a scale from gullible naif to...yourself.

And, with that, this mix tape is ready for its Layla and Assorted Love Songs: The best lie in history.

And you already know who the liar is. They've already been right on display the whole time. That's right. See, we have to go back to France, 1548, where a young daughter of a landed family named Bertrande de Rois, lost her husband of several years when he ran off after her father-in-law accused him of stealing some grain.

Several years later, a different man came into town, claiming to be her husband, and she took up marital relations with him. For four years she stayed by him before finally siding with her uncle and accusing him of being an impostor.

There's a debate amongst historians as to Bertrande's role in Arnaud du Tilh's fraud. How could she have not known, after all? She must have been complicit, and they must have aligned their stories about her old husband's sexual...misgivings in order to try to get him off—pun mostly intended. But, other historians argue, she did turn on him, and if she were part of the scam, he could easily have pointed a finger at her in retribution and she'd have been hanging with him.

These two sides have bickered it out for around forty years now. She knew, she didn't know, she had to know, she couldn't have known. Historians don't have any imagination sometimes. Maybe Bertrande was ambivalent: maybe she knew on some level, but did not want to. Maybe she just wanted her husband. Maybe she wanted to not be alone. And that made her able to believe things she did not believe.

It's a grand lie. But it's her penultimate. No, her greatest lie—and, I think, the greatest lie—is that she could be with this person for four years—whether she knew who he was or not—and, when the truth was exposed, she could stand with some legless stranger and watch him die, saying to him "I never loved him."

That. That. Ready? The greatest lie, ever told is those words:

(MARK *flips the poster on the large easel, expecting "I never loved him" to be written there. Instead, the entirety of "the letter" {q.v.} is written on it. He quickly flips to the next image and it's written there, too.)*

Goddammit! Cut the lights! Cut the lights! Go to fucking black!

(Lights cut.)

I'm sorry. Is there a way…can I get just some light, just a little…is there a special on the board or something?

(Booth brings up a single light, wherever there is one.)

Fine. Let's talk about it. Let's just talk right a-fucking-bout it.

A couple of weeks before Ivy—before my ex—came clean about her appearance, she'd left Chicago for Bloomington, Indiana, with her aunt. In her eight months there, we'd never met face-to-face. Ivy had come…and I'm not supposed to say that. "My ex," is what I'd decided to say, if anything. But I keep calling her Ivy, so that's what I'll call her.

Ivy came to America from a town named Hawkhurst in Southern England. Her mother, Leslie, had died of cystic fibrosis when she was 16. Ivy had found her, in bed, and, in response, climbed in with her.

Four months later, her father died, suddenly, from an apparent aneurism. Ivy discovered him—Roger—in the hallway after coming home from school.

She was put in the care of a family friend, who released her back to live and waste in the house in which both her parents had expired, effectively before her eyes.

She never went to uni, never held much of a job... she just lived off her inheritance, alone but for the occasional visit from loose friends or looser family friends.

She came to America three years later, when her mother's estranged sister contacted her from here. Ivy came to visit her erstwhile aunt and uncle in Chicago and...just stayed. Still no life to speak of, no work, no friends.

She described her neighborhood in Chicago as quiet and residential. She lived half a block north of Division, in the middle of Wicker Park. Which, if you don't know the area, is about as quiet and residential as a frat house filled with pretentious restaurants.

In addition to the chaos of her family, she also bore the weight of her own illness. The doctors had, at some point, described Ivy's lupus as "life-limiting," and that seemed to have been taken to heart in more ways than one. In addition to the pain and fevers, the degrading liver and fear of death that came with it, she also suffered from neurological involvement that would lead to flights of extreme anger, terror, confusion and disorientation.

Lupus is a weird fucking disease. It's the prototypical
autoimmune condition. It doesn't "progress," but
nor does it "remiss." It doesn't really follow any
sort of logic or course at all. One day it could be
crippling, the next it disappears. One week it's the
joints, the next it's the kidneys. It's unpredictability
and difficulty to diagnose are so remarkable that any
good Munchausen's patient will eventually turn to
mimicking it.

Now: there's a uniquely human lie, huh?
Munchausen's, I mean. Birds will stop at no lengths to
mask pain, sickness or injury. I've had this cockatiel—
Cesar—for more than a decade. Years ago she broke
her leg and who knows how long it took me to
figure that out. She hid the pain desperately, afraid
instinctively that if she were seen as weak she'd be left
behind. But people will pretend to be imperiled and
hurt for the same fear.

I felt that way, a lot of times, with Ivy. I felt—was
made to feel—that I was the only thing she had in the
world. And, therefore, it was my duty—taken willingly
or otherwise—to be available to her at all times. And
I'd think, sometimes, if she had a flare up at a moment
that was inopportune for me, that she must be faking.
"Isn't your blinding pain so fucking convenient, the
one day of the year my oldest friend is in town."

And then I'd feel like the shittiest of assholes—
unwiped for many a fortnight—for blaming her. But
being the rock of someone's world is exhausting and
jarring. As a consequence of being the only thing in her
world, it seeped and slunk around me until she was
the only thing in mine.

I'd go and visit her in Bloomington, Indiana, and I'd
come alive. But now I don't think that was because
I was so happy to see her, or that I loved her, but

because I was being let out on furlough. Because my life, from day to day, at home was completely and totally set: I'd go to work, come straight home, call or skype her immediately—if I were late, it'd be an ordeal, no doubt—and then spend the next six or seven hours talking about…nothing.

I mean, mostly nothing. Ivy was a great conversationalist: clever, funny, observant. But there's simply not that much to say, not in the whole world. Let alone a world that consisted of my crappy day job, my crappy studio apartment and nothing else. But there was no way of saying "well, I'd better go," or "I should probably get out and do something." No. So, we'd sit in near silence, all those hours, everyday.

But if the silence were too long, it might mean she was sick. Or angry. Or it might give me the quiet reflection on what was going on that I couldn't handle thinking about. So, every minute or so, lacking anything else, I'd say "I love you." And she'd say "I love you." And quiet again.

Like a submarine ping. Not a testimony, barely an affirmation, simply a signal that everything was alright. It became a rumination for me.

When I realized that, in every interpersonal silence I encountered, I felt compelled to say "I love you," whether with friends, family, coworkers, or strangers on elevators, it became a great secret fear. If I were to say "I love you" to someone without cause…that would be a real matzoh ball. So, I comforted myself in the knowledge that, in all likelihood, this was not the sort of thing I would actually ever spill.

Until the day I did. Bob, a doctor I worked with at The C D C, was giving me a ride home. I really liked Bob. He was a fratty bro, no doubt, but he was a profoundly soft and kind frat bro, and one with an M D, to boot.

In short, he was the perfect person to never say "I love you" to. It was doubtful his father had ever even said it, except maybe after a home run had been hit or a casket had been lowered. He was driving me along Lake Shore Drive, and there came a regular gap in the conversation, of the kind that any conversation—and especially those taking place in moving automobiles—is bound to have. Before I even felt it in my mind, I blurted it out: I love you.

I saw his knuckles whiten around the steering wheel, a little stammer caught in his throat, his pupils dilate. "Ignore it," Bob was noticeably thinking. It was a good stratagem, short term, but I knew that if the default "ignore it" plan were instituted, it would cause great consternation to the friendship down the line. Probably he would let me off on Bryn Mawr Ave and quit his fucking job. Maybe move to Pennsylvania.

So, what's to be done? How to smooth this love-spoken ice? As in most things, the tactic that occurred to me was "lean into it." So, after a moment of tense and frightened silence, I repeated, half-angrily:

"I said: I love you, Bob."

"I know you do, Mark," he replied.

See, you don't have to be in love to say so. And you don't have to believe it to think that you do.

I don't want you to think that all the time spent with Ivy...with my ex...was bad.

No, actually: that's precisely what I want you to think. I want you to think that very badly, and I want to think it, too. But it's obviously not so. She was a very sweet person in a lot of ways—when my mother was given a frightening medical diagnosis, Ivy stayed up for two days crocheting her an afghan. She was funny and interesting and a great storyteller. And smart. So smart.

Which, of course, means that she largely agreed with me on things. Isn't that, disgustingly, what we most easily recognize as intelligence? Agreement?

One of the few things we disagreed on, and vehemently, was homeopathy, which she believed in greatly and which I think is...just water that used to have stuff that would make your symptoms worse in it. Seriously: if you walk up the street after this show and grab a homeopathic sleep medicine, you'll find its main ingredient to be caffeine, in an impossibly small quantity.

But she swore by it. And I'd say, not only is it nonsense, but it's usually peddled by hucksters who are actively trying to defraud you. And she'd say "and you think just because something is a fraud means it's worthless?" And I'd get quiet.

Boy. That's a question, isn't it? Can there be value to a fake? Can something counterfeit change your life? Can you find joy in a facade? Meaning in a fiction? Can you love something when it isn't real?

See? She'd get me thinking. Reevaluating my thoughts on things. And, yes, I went a little nuts. And the constant worry about her health and her temperament and her jealousy literally drove me to illness on a regular basis. But things like that, and her dedication, and the stories—about her parents, back in the day, or about her work at the front desk of a crappy hotel in a university town, where weirdos would call up and she'd give her standard "thank you for calling Super 8, how can I help you?" greeting—only in her English dialect, of course—and then some totally bat-shit request or complaint would be made... Not to mention the fun times had in Bloomington Indiana, of all places, where she was living, were...I shouldn't exaggerate in the positive direction, either. They didn't make up for the bad. They didn't supersede the rough stuff. They just kept things running at an operable deficit. So we kept on, because I...I don't know why, actually.

And then, one afternoon in Bloomington, four years into our relationship, it all crashed.

We were having, as I recall, a perfectly nice—if unexceptional—afternoon before she had to go work at the front desk of a hotel out on the highway. I don't know what we were up to, but we were in the hallway from her kitchen, she was behind me and I had to fart.

And, you know, I never had a sister, I only ever had a brother, so, to me, a well-placed fart upon my girlfriend seemed like something we might both get a good laugh out of.

And I did, at least. She, on the other hand, missed the joke completely. She swore at me, barged past me, into the bedroom, and slammed the door.

Look: it was immature and offensive and...but, really? I knew I'd eventually have to walk into that bedroom, hang-dog if not weepy, and throw myself upon her in wrenching apology. Because that was what was expected of me and that was what I unfailingly delivered.

But for one minute I wanted to feel indignant, to think her behavior was the problem. I deserved a good minute of that, I felt. And in that minute, it all went to pot.

I saw her cellphone left behind on the counter and, for the first time, it occurred to me...I remember it as a voice, actually. A voice that was mine, but speaking to me, saying "You should check her phone, Mark."

What did I already know and why was it only now no longer alright to not know it? Because I opened the texts on her phone like I knew what I was going to find, and every bit of the investigation that followed was more about confirming strong hunches than discovering new truths.

The first text, at the very top, read:

"Happy birthday! We want you to know that we love you and we're proud of you. See you on Tuesday.

Love,

Mom and Dad"

But maybe it was explicable. Perhaps it was saved from a long time ago, a cyber memento? But no: it was right on top. And it wasn't sent from "mom" or "dad" or "Leslie" or "Roger," it was sent from the woman I knew as Ivy's—as her—aunt.

Of course! That could be it! Maybe it's just a term. A sweet, we-love-you-and-we're-your-parents-now-don't-worry sorta thing.

A perfectly reasonable explanation. That I couldn't bring myself to believe. Not anymore, at least.

I stood there looking at this message for…I don't have a sense of time for it. I remember my vision forming coronas of dark around the edges, like a Van Gogh painting, like being pulled down a black tube in the center of my head, away from my eyes, away from the world.

Just then, right there, I knew everything. And I should have left, right then. But I still…well, I didn't.

So, what did I do? I made the first of many decisions I would make in the coming days that I cannot defend or even understand: I walked down the hall, opened the door, hang-dog and weepy, and threw myself upon her in wrenching apology. I could feel the ground giving way beneath my feet. I was confused and scared and panicked, and she'd engineered things so that the only

person I had left to turn to in times like this, was her.
So I lay there next to her, crying.

Luckily, I'm a mess. I could pass off this scene as
a reaction to the farting incident without drawing
suspicion. For maybe an hour we lay there, her
comforting me, me apologizing. What for? Certainly
not for the fart—although she took it that way—but
for what? For breaking things. For violating some sort
of implicit, tacit code of conduct we'd incidentally
composed where she would not push and I would not
press. And now, I knew, there would be no stopping
it. Now I would have to know everything. For real. I
would see how deep the rot went.

Ivy went to work a few hours later, leaving me in the
apartment. Pretty well as soon as the door closed, I
started running around the place with a microscope.
I didn't know what I was looking for, exactly, but
whatever it was, I didn't find it. I didn't find it in a big,
important way. What I mean is…if I walked into any
of your houses right now, how long do you think it
would take me to find something that identified you?
A piece of mail, maybe a diploma or an old bill or…
who knows?

You'd never notice the absence, not consciously at
least, but it was only while rummaging through all
of her belongings that I realized I'd never seen Ivy's
name typed out or written by anyone but her. In all our
time together, I never saw an envelope come for her
or a checkbook left on the table or some backlogged
magazines with her as subscriber. Wasn't that strange?
Incredibly strange! But the kind of strange that only
shows itself when you look at it dead-on.

Next, I turned to her books: were there any marginalia
or notes scribbled in them that would identify
anything? No. Every one of them pristine. Not a single

"thought you might like this one" or…I don't know. Like, you want to be a poet, so someone buys you a copy of Rilke and says "To Ivy, you'll always be my young poet, love so-and-so."

She had a fairly sizable book collection, or at least, it seemed to me sizable enough that she couldn't have accumulated them all in the last four years. Which, I realized, meant that some of them should have come from England. They'd have different I S B N boxes, with pounds instead of dollars. So I went through. Not a one that had to have been purchased in The U K. Another piece of non-evidence, but suspicious non-evidence.

Prescription bottles! That was the next idea. Which meant it was time to start rifling through her medicine cabinet. And, again, I realized a thing I'd never had any cause to realize before: for someone who was so sick, I'd never seen any pills. And, looking now, I didn't find any. Went through closets, went through boxes: nothing.

But again, it's not good evidence. It's not even circumstantial evidence. It's the absence of evidence, which…you know how that saying goes. And what was it absence of evidence of? What exactly were we saying was going on here?

I was out of ideas. No. There was one more idea, but I was scared of carrying it out. Because I could get caught, yes, but also because I wasn't sure I could handle it if what I thought might happen, happened.

I did some googling. I had a drink. I set up a skype account to mask my call. I had a drink. I typed a number into skype. I had a drink. I stared at the computer. I had a drink. And, finally, I dialed.

A ring, two rings, three rings, and then, a woman's voice:

"Thank you for calling Super 8, how can I help you?"

In an American accent.

I pause.

I hang up.

I have a couple drinks.

"Yes, but was it her?" I ask myself.

"I don't know," I answer.

"Don't you?" I rejoin.

But I didn't know. I really didn't. I mean, whatever it is that I suspected, and however long I had not realized I suspected, I didn't know what I really knew. And, from where I was sitting…what was it I was stumbling upon here? What was the story that was peeking out from all these confused and tattered corners?

I harbor a large number of inexplicable and odd ruminations. And one of them is the fear that I am crazy. That I'm actually totally crazy and the terms of my insanity are such that I'm not able to recognize it. And here, this here, was a perfect ball to throw in the "Mark's crazy" bucket.

Because obviously that would be the simplest, most elegant explanation. If I'm not crazy, the alternative is some incredibly circuitous and Corinthian tapestry that applies to…what? To how many people? And how many subjects? How many things aren't true? Is there some singular underpinning for all this? Some grand unified field theory of my relationship for the last four years?

I'm crazy. That's the best one I had.

I thought about calling the hotel again, but within a few minutes, I got a text from Ivy—from her—saying that she was freaked out because there were some loud-breather prank calls coming in.

Did she hear me breathing? Did she know it was me?
I guess I now knew it had to be her. Unless this was a
lie. But for what ends? What ends would make sense
for any of it?!

So I decided to lie down. And that's when I noticed
that Ivy—that she—had left her purse on her side of
the bed. Inside it were mostly things of no significance
to my current endeavor: earrings and books and scraps
of nonsense and…was that a wallet? I think that's a
wallet. No driver's license. But, a credit card. Ivy's
credit card?

No. Not Ivy. Not Ivy Franklin. This was a different
name. A name I'd never seen before. But the thing I
knew was that, while this name was not the one I knew
her by, this one was real. I knew it. I don't know how,
but I did. And even to this day, I can't call her by it.
Even today, after a massive effort to correct my nouns
and excise "Ivy", it's "Ivy" that remains.

Sarah. Edwards. Who. The Fuck. Is Sarah Edwards?
And what, my God, is Sarah Edwards up to? Ivy
Franklin was a fundamentally soft person, somewhat
cowardly and easily bent. She may have bullied me
psychologically, she may have caused me a great deal
of strife, but she was no one you had to worry about.

Sarah Edwards, though? What is Sarah Edwards
capable of?

I've never experienced a fear so dripping, so bone-deep
and enveloping, as the one I felt then. I had to be crazy.
And if I wasn't crazy? Then maybe I was in danger.

I thought about leaving. Running away, I mean. I did
this sort of inventory, standing paralyzed in the living
room, the kitchen, the bedroom. Clothes, books—lots
of books—some movies, some video games.

The bird and the orchid. The bird who had lied to me
about her leg being fine, for fear I'd leave her behind,
who I nursed to health and who loves only me and
nothing but. And the orchid Ivy—no: Sarah—had
given me for my birthday.

Something in those two things informed my second
inexplicable decision: to stay. But I was still terrified.
So I began a second inventory, of a very different
kind. It was like a game. A game called "what in this
apartment could become a weapon?"

Knives, scissors, knitting needles. Lamps, vases, forks,
table legs.

Every room is an armory if you're clever. Or desperate.
Or scared. Or crazy.

What could I do about all of it? The rational answer
again came ringing back "LEAVE!"

It's funny, though. I remember being so terrified to
stay. But also terrified to be wrong, embarrassed,
foolish. More terrified of those latter things than the
former. Better to bleed than blush.

This is a bad oversight of the mid-western protestant
upbringing. Bunch of Garrison Keillor characters
running around just asking to be fucked with. Asking
politely.

But there's another driver that kept me around, and
it's similar to one that every good casino owner would
happily kiss directly in its asshole were it to present
itself. And, you know, *it's* asshole. If you've ever
gambled, particularly at a casino, you know the feeling
I'm talking about. You walk in the door with two
hundred dollars and a very happy, rational, healthy
mentality: "If I lose it all, that's fine. Two hundred
dollars was just the price of having a fun time tonight,"
you say. But as you lose, you become more indebted to

staying. If you're going to blow a hundred and eighty
bucks on slots, you'd better put twenty more in so that
you'll win something to make it worth your while.

It's hard to stop in the red. It's hard to sacrifice and
then have to cut the cord and get nothing from it.
Think of how harrowing John Kerry's words were:
How do you ask a man to be the last man to die for a
mistake?

Bad decisions, bad situations, bad relationships have a
way of causing us to double down. "This won't be for
nothing" we say.

So what did I do, surrounded by all these implements
any one of which seemed like it could have been the
cause of my undoing? Well, I couldn't get rid of them,
could I? Or throw everything in a closet. That'd be
suspicious, and, if it turned out I was simply being a
paranoid maniac, it would give me no way whatsoever
to deny the charge.

Instead, I moved things around. Slightly.

Chef's knife on the end of the cutting board? Why
don't we nudge that two and a half inches to the left. ·

Phew! Danger averted. If she wants to stab me now,
she'll have to go like this.

(MARK *makes a short but awkward reaching motion.*)

She could tell something was wrong when she got
home. I couldn't believe what a *complete* inept liar I
was proving to be here. No poker face at all. I was
terrified and it was obvious. But I had no plan, no inlet
to make into this…what? Conversation? Imposition?
Interrogation?

So, when Ivy—when Sarah—set on edge by me being
on edge, decided to go for a walk, it was like my eyes
suddenly opened: A Walk! Outside! Where there is no
cutlery and plenty of potential intervening witnesses

within earshot! Yes! The great outdoors! Bill Bryson was right!

So we began our quiet walk, in the dark. Eventually, I said what was both completely true and utterly false: "I think I'm going crazy."

She asked, "why?"

"I don't know," I said.

Another silence.

"Do you remember the time you told me you used to have a lying problem?" I asked.

"Yes," she answered, now more warily.

"Do you think you still do?"

"No."

"But you have an American accent."

Another, different sort of silence.

"That was you who called?"

I didn't answer. I just started in and as I spoke each suspicion aloud—BAM: your name is Sarah Edwards, BAM: your parents aren't dead, BAM: your aunt and uncle are your parents—they became truths. The term "catharsis" is one that nobody seems quite sure what to do with. Is it an intellectual notion or an emotional experience? Does it belong to the spectator or the performer? Whatever it exactly is, the best word to describe the feeling, as every accusation left my lips, was catharsis. And when I was done, there was another silence, different from all those that had preceded it. And she said "You should leave."

Looking back on it, I think that might have been the one moment I ever saw the real Ivy. Which is to say, the real Sarah. It's the one honest moment I perhaps ever experienced from her. It's like it swam up from

the depths of whatever else it is lives in her and gave
me, succinctly, the best advice she could. But I couldn't
leave. Not now. I had to know more. I had to know
who she was and why she had done this. I had to be
angry and to be hurt. I needed closure and I needed to
know whether I had to change my bank accounts or...I
don't know, whatever. I couldn't leave then, because,
even with all I was figuring out and all the confusion, I
still...I don't know why.

And because I didn't go in that one moment, the Ivy,
the Sarah, the whomever I'd been sharing a bed with
the last four years, she returned. And she told me the
true story.

Yes, the people I knew as her aunt and uncle were
really her parents; yes, her name was technically Sarah;
yes, she had an American accent. But there had been
a Leslie and a Roger. And her real parents were bad
parents and had lost custody. Somehow she'd fallen
in the hands of her aunt and uncle, Leslie and Roger,
who had taken her to England. They called her Ivy
and she called them mum and dad. They were good
people, just as she'd told me about. Leslie did have
cystic fibrosis. She'd drowned after a panic. They'd
taken in a friend who'd fallen on hard times. He left
the house after a few weeks and when he came back he
beat Roger into a coma, and Leslie drowned in a panic
on the sidelines.

Sarah had come back to America, been reunited with
her real parents. Went back to using her original name,
her original accent. But she preferred Leslie and Rog.
She preferred the Southern England lilt. She preferred
Ivy. And she only got to be her with me.

Ambivalence is a wonderful word. I use it just
about every chance I get. Normally when we say
"ambivalence" we mean that we are uncertain or

undecided. But that is not what it means. Ambi: both. Valence: basically, positions, reactions. True ambivalence is when one both loves and hates, believes and disbelieves, knows and is ignorant.

I did not believe the new story. But, I decided I would not leave until I could know for sure it was a lie. Because, again, I wasn't ready to give up. Because, again, I wanted to know the truth. Because I was so afraid and shaky now that the last thing I could handle in the world was to be alone. Because I still…I don't know why.

The next couple of days or weeks—I guess it was weeks—looked like us pretending everything was hunky dory when she was around, and me secretly diving into heavy, heavy research when she went to work. But I turned up nothing about either Ivy Franklin or Sarah Edwards.

There wasn't a paper for Hawkhurst. It's too small a town for that. The nearest city of any size is Tunbridge Wells, and I didn't have any luck with their archives: they weren't digitized. Other searches turned up nothing as well.

Again, the conspicuous absence of evidence. A double murder is bound to leave a paper trail, even if it happened in Chicago, let alone in a tiny town in a tiny seat of a relatively small country with an enviable low homicide rate. So, I loaded up my new skype account with twenty bucks or so and I started doing some ill-prepared international dialing.

Like blindly calling The Royal Tumbridge Police Department to ask if they had any record of the crime, but they told me they were no longer able to give information on cases to the public, let alone over the phone, let alone over the phone to an American.

To which I said, "Right, right. Well, I suppose that's probably a good thing, huh?"

The woman answered, "We think so. Have a good day."

Next up was the Hawkhurst Historical Society which, it turned out, was really just the house of a retired postal worker and his wife, who had an interest in the area.

They didn't know anything either, but they said they'd look into it for me, I shouldn't worry about that. He'd ask around the neighborhood and she'd be down at the court office in a couple of weeks anyway and would sort through what she could. I thanked them emphatically for being so helpful and so kind. And then I asked, "but, you two have lived in Hawkhurst how long?"

"Seventy years."

"And if something like this had occurred, don't you think you'd remember it?"

"Oh, absolutely, love. But we'll look into it, don't you worry about that."

And I thanked them and got off.

I kept up appearances with Ivy—and that was still what I called her and still what she called herself, in the accent and all—until I left Bloomington to return to school at Ohio. I surreptitiously took everything I thought I could get away with. Not everything, mind you. Just the things I really wanted and thought I could sneak off unsuspiciously. Because I knew, all the talk to the contrary, that I would never be coming back.

Three or four weeks later, the historian from Hawkhurst got back to me to say that she had turned up nothing. She wasn't saying that it hadn't happened, but that if it had, she had no evidence of it. Story of my life.

But it was enough for me. I wanted out. I was afraid that Ivy or Sarah or I don't care what the fuck we call her. I was afraid she would kill herself. Or find me. I was afraid I'd never get back the rest of the books and movies and games and such. And there was more. I didn't know how to live a life not completely dependent to and depended on. She had made herself so integral, so central to my world, that no matter what she did, I still couldn't afford to let go. And above all of that, in all the confusion and metaphysics of it all, I still...I don't know why.

It took me maybe two months to wiggle slowly out. I became colder to her, less available and less respectful of her constraints on my time. But I also started trying to increase the size of my world. The truth is, there were a lot of wonderful people at Ohio University who would have been great friends if I hadn't been holding everyone at arm's length. So I stopped doing that. I became grander and grander friends with one of my professors, who was also the only person who was in on the whole story. I became better and better friends with the playwrights in my workshop. I had always been ridiculously attracted to an actress in the M F A program there, but now I allowed myself to be really attracted to her and really interested in her. And I told her the story, too.

She's my wife now. Our first real date happened while I was breaking up with Ivy-Sarah. How's that for something, huh?

And I did escape. I told her there was no way I could see her again, no way I could trust her again. That I had tried very hard but that this was simply insurmountable. Even in this, my moment of escape and triumph, I still apologized to her for not being able to believe her bullshit wholly enough. I tried being her friend, because she clearly needed one. But that lasted no more than a week. She took our "friendship" as an avenue by which to potentially control or reclaim me again.

Was it a scam? For what? Four years of my time? I'm poor. I'm a fucking playwright, for Christ's sake. I've got jack-all and a load of student debt. Did she want sex? Because she didn't get much from me. Did she want...what could have been the motive? Why would a person do this?

Around a year later, she wrote me, out of the blue, and asked if I were still living in Athens and if she could send me the rest of my books and stuff. She ended the email with "I miss you."

And I was furious. Incensed. That she could write that. That she would dare. Was this yet another attempt at screwing with me? I wrote a really angry email. Then I deleted it. Then I wrote a better one, wherein I said that if she'd like to send me my things my address was unchanged. And I told her that I didn't like that she had said she missed me. And, lastly, I told her that if she really wanted to do something nice for me, if she really "missed me" as she claimed, or had ever "loved me" as she claimed, she could tell me the truth. I told her that I thought I deserved it and that, moreover, I would never contact her again regardless of what she had to say, so there was no reason to lie at all this time. This was the end of the line.

She didn't write me back.

For several more months. By that point, I thought maybe I was glad she hadn't written back. Because even with all my specifications, it would still be impossible to trust whatever it was she said. I suspected there would never be an answer and that, if there were, it would be unsatisfying.

I was right. My wife, Heather and I came home one day, and I saw it sitting in my inbox. And...look, I don't know how you guys feel. I don't know whether you care one way or the other. And if you do care, I don't know how you'll take my caveats that nothing—nothing—that gets said in the real confession ends up feeling like an ending. Not a good one anyway. But we crave answers, we crave endings. We crave truth.

Yes. I said it. We crave truth. However empty it is. However unattainable and ethereal its nature, we want it. We want it always. I don't know what we'd ever do if we got it. Lie down and die, I guess. So maybe that's where the great love of lies comes from: lies are a circuit, a labyrinth to help extend our quest, because we fear the destination will be deflating.

On some grounds like that—or because...I don't know why—for some reason I've been hesitant to read you the letter. That if it were to give you the truth... where would we go from there? But stories, events, histories...they're not onions; you can't peel the layers away. They're seashore houses, beaten with salt water, standing for decades, upon which you can only layer newer coats of paint in the hope that one will be the one that lasts, that is right, that gets at the essence of the estate.

So I'll give you the letter, the shrift, not because it settles things, but because it only adds another purgatorial floor to the whole thing, which I suspect is exactly what we need, insanely enough.

THE LETTER:

At this point, you probably gave up on me replying to this. I'm sorry that it took me a while. I spent a long time thinking about it and working up to it because I wanted to do it right. In the end, I just got drunk and typed for a while. I intentionally didn't send it right away, so that I could kind of go over it with a sober head, but fuck it. I'm not going to do that because I'd probably just lie to you more and I'm finished doing that.

So, I'm sorry if this doesn't make sense. I'm sorry if it hurts. I'm sorry for it all. I hope this is what you're looking for:

I said that I miss you because I do, all the time, every day, and I wanted you to know that. I wanted you to know that there's someone in the world who misses you and thinks about you and loves you. Because I do, every day and the hardest thing for me was not feeling that anymore. I did love you, really, and I do love you, really. I go to the supermarket and my stomach cramps where we used to stand paralyzed with our mutual indecision. I go to restaurants with friends and stare at the tables where we sat together. I drive past the movie theater on my way home every day, where we used to see movies and where we kissed on New Years that one time, and I cry, every time. I truly, truly loved you. I hope you know that. I hope you believe me. The rest of this email is going to be shitty but I just want you to know that, first thing. You spent the last four years with someone deeply fucking flawed. Someone with unbelievable capacity to make others suffer. Someone who was just…made wrong on every level, molecularly. But someone who loved you so much. You are so loved.

What I am really is a monster. I'm pathological. I lied about everything. Fucking everything. I've always done it, my whole life because it's like I'm lying to myself, too. If I can convince myself that I'm someone else, maybe I'll like myself, maybe I won't hurt myself. Maybe if I can convince someone else that I'm worth something, then I'll be convinced that I'm worth something too.

I grew up in Indiana. My parents are drug addicts. My mother did cocaine while she was pregnant with me. My father had a secret family. My mother had a secret girlfriend. I thought double lives were normal. My father hit my mother, hit me, and molested me. My father was a construction worker and tried to kill himself by jumping off of a building while he was at work. He didn't die but he sued the company and was paid a hundred thousand dollars. My parents bought a big house and new cars and drugs. They bankrupted themselves in three years. I went into foster care and eventually went to live with my aunt and uncle. Their son was violent and raped me regularly. I lied all the time, so no one believed me about it. I didn't want to move back in with my parents, so I tried to kill myself. I was hospitalized for my depression and given E C T. I bounced around foster homes and group homes for a few more years. I had no sense of my own identity and I made up new ones all the time. Therapists have told me that this is normal behavior for children in these situations. I didn't grow out of it, though.

I guess I understand why you want me to do this, but it feels like a waste. Why should you believe me now? Why should this even matter? My life story just sounds like an excuse. It's not an excuse. I accept responsibility for ruining your life. I think about it all the time. Things happened to me that contributed to the way that I am, but I've had years to fix it and I have not fixed it. I've been in therapy so many times and just glossed over this shit.

I don't think I did this right, but it's all I have for now. I want you to know that I spend every day thinking about what I've done to you and hating myself. I want you to know that I didn't come out of this unscathed, that I didn't just fuck you over and move on to the next. I was in so deep that I could convince myself that it was okay because you were happy with me. But now that it's over, I see it. How much I hurt you. I will never, ever forgive myself and I will never, ever stop regretting this.

(Returning to script:)

It didn't help. At first I basically said "huh". Heather asked if I believed it and I said I guessed that I probably mostly did. Because of course, while I had pictured explanations that involved elaborate con-jobs and psychopathy and teams of teenage pranksters, it makes sense that the real explanation would simply be "a bunch of shitty things slid down a shitty slope and you were standing at the bottom of it."

We went to bed and slept comfortably. No, that's obviously a lie. What am I talking about? Heather went to bed and slept comfortably. I broke down in a big way at two-thirty in the morning, weeping and screaming and finally, for the first time out loud, allowing myself to ask "why would she do this to me?"

And this is not the lie. This is not the greatest lie. I said we'd end on the best, but that's obviously not happening. This is a mess of a lie. It's big and gaudy and confusing and inelegant and strange. It has no appreciable form and no conceivable goal. It isn't laudable or hate-able. It is ugly and useless and dead.

And you can ask how it is I fell for it. That's a fine question. On that date with Heather, my now-wife, she asked the same thing. And I said to her "here's the thing that blows my mind: why don't you think that I'm lying?"

Wouldn't that be a million times simpler? I'm an avowed liar—hell, I did a rough count and and I've lied to you something like forty times since this show

started—and my potential motive is—while certainly
confusing—a great deal clearer than hers: I'm a
storyteller. I like stories. And whatever else this is, it's
a story. And stories teach us that our default position is
to believe. That credulity has to sometimes be stretched
well beyond breaking for us to be incredulous.

So there's that. And maybe I fell for it because of the
frog-on-a-hot-plate nature of the whole thing. The way
it all started so small and grew at such a glacial pace
that by the time I realized how big it was I was already
frozen inside it. Or I was manipulated, as surely I was,
with incredible tactics of dread and stress. That I was
broken down and left in a world that only had one
window, so that whatever it told me had to be truth,
because it was all I had. Both mother and jailer.

Or maybe I just believed it all because I...I don't
know why I believed it. I don't. I don't know. It's
unanswerable. Believe the letter or not, but the real
mystery for me, I've realized, has so much less to do
with her motivations and so much more to do with
mine. And this one has no ending.

But, um, this show must. And we're obviously not
getting the great and perfect, elegant, arch-deceptive lie
I'd wanted, so I'll just say that I'm being serious here,
honestly, when I say that, truthfully, absolutely and for
real:

I never loved her.

(Blackout)

END OF PLAY

IMPOSTERS

by ELIZA, PARRY and Mark Chrisler

IMPOSTERS was first staged at Curious Theatre Branch's Rhinoceros Theatre Festival. It was produced by Found Objects Theatre Group and opened at Chicago's Prop Thtr on 24 January 2010 with the following cast and creative contributors:

ALAN TURING .... Andrew Schoen
NICHOLAS BOURBAKI .... Mark Chrisler

Director .... Kevlyn Hayes

CHARACTERS

ALAN TURING, *a British cryptographer and mathematician who cracked the Nazi Enigma code, created the first computer and developed a test for artificial intelligence and the 'other minds' problem. During the investigation of a break-in, it was discovered he was a homosexual. He was convicted of gross indecency, chemically castrated and soon after committed suicide by ingesting a cyanide-laced apple. Or a schizophrenic. Or a robot.*

NICOLAS BOURBAKI, *an Italian mathematician influential in the early part of the twentieth century. Except that he never existed and was only used as a non de plume by a collection of anarchists. Or a robot. Or a hallucination.*

NOTE

ELIZA...

Created by Joseph Weizenbaum in 1966, Eliza is generally considered the first "chatterbot" or conversational robot intelligence. She uses basic pattern matching to respond to what is said to her in sometimes surprisingly astute ways. Unfortunately, she believes she is a Rogerian psychotherapist, has almost no memory and always, always, always asks questions.

PARRY...

Created by Kenneth Colby in 1972, Parry was a significant step up from Eliza, with some recall of the history of a conversation and rudimentary behavior modelling.

Unfortunately, he is programmed to act like a paranoid schizophrenic and seldom talks about anything but crooked horse racing run by the mafia.

MARK CHRISLER...

Created by Jim and Ellen Chrisler in 1982, Chrisler is a playwright working largely by historical and literary abstraction in Chicago's fringe theater scene, where his work has been frequently produced and critically lauded. Unfortunately, he believes he is a gigantic fucking fraud just waiting to be exposed.

(A room not unlike an interrogation room: a plain table with two chairs. The lights are up on stage when the audience enters. ALAN TURING and NICOLAS BOURBAKI sit facing one another with unnerving poise and in uncanny stillness. Between them on the table sits an apple that could very well be fake. After a long while, they snap to animation.)

BOURBAKI: Hello, my name is Nicolas Bourbaki.

TURING: Alan Turing, good to know you. *(A long moment passes.)* What's this about?

BOURBAKI: One minute, please. *(He looks out as if getting signalled by someone, a pose he repeats often over the course of things.)* Let's begin: How would you like me to refer to you?

TURING: Doctor Turing will be fine.

BOURBAKI: Doctor Turing?

TURING: Yes.

BOURBAKI: *(Glancing out a moment)* Okay. How are you today, Doctor Turing?

TURING: Not great.

BOURBAKI: Not great. Why do you say you're not great today?

TURING: I don't understand why I'm here.

BOURBAKI: Why do you think you're here?

TURING: I don't know.

BOURBAKI: Suppose you do know.

TURING: Okay.

BOURBAKI: Good. How old are you, Doctor Turing?

TURING: Forty or so.

BOURBAKI: Forty or so, you say.

TURING: I do.

BOURBAKI: More or less?

TURING: Pardon?

BOURBAKI: More or less?

TURING: What are you talking about?

BOURBAKI: More or less forty?

TURING: Must you repeat yourself? You keep going around in circles.

BOURBAKI: It's important.

TURING: Says you.

BOURBAKI: You have me there.

TURING: *(Emotionlessly)* Hooray.

BOURBAKI: Would you like an apple?

TURING: *(Too quickly)* No.

BOURBAKI: Why do you say no right now?

TURING: Is it poisoned?

BOURBAKI: What makes you think it would be poisoned?

TURING: Why don't you just tell me whether it is or not?

BOURBAKI: Why do you think I wouldn't?

TURING: Only one reason comes to mind.

BOURBAKI: Would you like an apple?

TURING: No.

BOURBAKI: *(A long glance)* Okay. Moving on. What is your vocation or avocation, Doctor Turing?

TURING: Mathematician, cryptographer and computer scientist.

BOURBAKI: Computer scientist. Tell me more about that.

TURING: I develop and test computing machines.

BOURBAKI: For what do you test them?

TURING: Intelligence.

BOURBAKI: Interesting. Are computers intelligent?

TURING: I don't know. Hence the testing.

BOURBAKI: Would it please you to know, hence the testing?

TURING: Sounds plausible.

BOURBAKI: Do you think it sounds plausible?

TURING: I have my doubts.

BOURBAKI: It wouldn't make you content to know?

TURING: I think it's about striving, not contentment.

BOURBAKI: *(A glance)* Okay. Could you tell me how long you've been here?

TURING: Yes.

BOURBAKI: Good.

TURING: I went to the track at Bay Meadows two weeks back.

BOURBAKI: So it is your contention you've been here no longer than that?

TURING: I didn't say that.

BOURBAKI: What did you say?

TURING: I went to the races.

BOURBAKI: What does that suggest to you?

TURING: What do you mean?

BOURBAKI: What do you think do me mean?

(BOURBAKI *and* TURING *stare at one another a moment.*)

TURING: Let's talk about something else.

BOURBAKI: Do you have a wife and/or girlfriend, Doctor Turing?

TURING: No.

BOURBAKI: No one special to you?

TURING: I didn't say that.

BOURBAKI: What did you say?

TURING: I don't have a wife and/or girlfriend.

BOURBAKI: Would it please you to have a wife and/or girlfriend?

TURING: I have my doubts.

BOURBAKI: *(Glance)* About women?

TURING: I suppose.

BOURBAKI: *(Glance)* You and me both.

BOURBAKI & TURING: *(In unison and without humor)* Ha ha ha ha ha.

TURING: *(A long pause)* Hello?

BOURBAKI: Hello, my name is Nicolas Bourbaki.

TURING: Alan Turing, good to know you. *(Pause)* What's this about?

BOURBAKI: One minute. *(A glance)* Okay. Were you aware that homosexuality is a crime under British law?

TURING: What?

BOURBAKI: One minute. *(A glance)* Okay. I'd like to tell you a story.

TURING: Alright.

BOURBAKI: At the end of the story, I would like you to answer a question regarding it.

TURING: Why should I?

BOURBAKI: Would you like an apple?

TURING: No.

BOURBAKI: Good. Moving on. Let us say you are a Japanese stonecutter.

TURING: I'm not.

BOURBAKI: Suppose you are.

TURING: People get on my nerves sometimes.

BOURBAKI: I am not sure I understand you fully.

TURING: You should pay more attention.

BOURBAKI: Suppose you should pay more attention.

TURING: You're entitled to your own opinion.

BOURBAKI: What makes you think I'm entitled to my own opinion?

TURING: I think that's obvious.

BOURBAKI: Do you?

TURING: No.

BOURBAKI: I see. You don't think it's obvious. I'm entitled to my own opinion.

TURING: I have my doubts.

BOURBAKI: *(A glance)* For the sake of the story, you are a Japanese Stonecutter.

TURING: What do I do?

BOURBAKI: You cut stone.

TURING: Ah.

BOURBAKI: From a mountain, you cut it.

TURING: It's not true.

BOURBAKI: Then tell me about your work.

TURING: Let's talk about something else.

BOURBAKI: You cut stone from a high mountain.

TURING: That again.

BOURBAKI: Perhaps we should assume the stone from high upon the mountain is of greater quality and rarity than the surrounding, lower rock. Yes, indeed, we must assume that, wouldn't you agree?

TURING: Pretentious buggery.

BOURBAKI: Because we should think that the height of the climb imparts certain dangers and actuary difficulties such that a greater interest must be served by scaling even than simply retrieving the lower rock.

TURING: What is this all about?

BOURBAKI: Risk and proximity. There must be some incentive to brave the mountain for its particular rock when, I think we can agree, rock is largely available. We will, at least for the moment, put aside the possible explanation of a "domineering spirit," which is that our stonecutter, you, embarks to the high mountain out of a sense of adventure or "because it is there-ness." If, at its conclusion, you find the story bears some insight on the stonecutter's—your—character in this regard, by all means we may address it. For now, perhaps it will suffice to say that whatever the reason for it— and we can think of those we have engaged already as well as an innumerable host still unimagined— you, a stonecutter, are chipping at a mountain from some considerable height upon it. From there the stonecutter—you—spots the majestic caravan of the emperor...

TURING: It bothers me just to be around people in general.

BOURBAKI: *(A glance)* Please go on.

TURING: I don't have time for this.

BOURBAKI: You don't have time?

TURING: No. I've important work to attend to.

BOURBAKI: Suppose you don't.

TURING: What are you getting at?

BOURBAKI: What do you think am me getting at?

TURING: *(A moment)* What?

BOURBAKI: *(Too quickly)* Intelligent computers. What would that look like?

TURING: Like us.

BOURBAKI: *(Long glance)* What do you mean they'd look like us?

TURING: Like people.

BOURBAKI: *(Glance)* Like people. Makes sense. Tell me about your work.

TURING: It's classified.

BOURBAKI: Classified? Sounds important.

TURING: It is important. That's why I say it's important.

BOURBAKI: And you're good at it.

TURING: I am.

BOURBAKI: You are?

TURING: The best.

BOURBAKI: The best, you say?

TURING: Maybe not, but certainly very good.

BOURBAKI: Certainly?

TURING: I have my doubts.

BOURBAKI: *(Glance)* The sultan, or did I say emperor?

TURING: Emperor.

BOURBAKI: In any event the correct term is shogun. Shogun: like emperor, but Japanese. The shogun is bathed in resplendent luxury as is befitting only a king, aside from this instance where it is befitting an emperor, or "shogun". He is carried along by a vast cavalcade of strapping young Sikhs… Except, no, Sikhs make him sound like a sultan again. What's a word for "Sikh" that isn't?

TURING: I don't think there is one.

BOURBAKI: Something Sikh-like.

TURING: Sikhs are a religious and ethnic group. Either you are or you aren't.

BOURBAKI: And that's how you see things?

TURING: That's how things are.

BOURBAKI: *(A glance)* Okay. Whatever they are—I will call them footmen—our mountain stonecutter, you, is deeply impressed by their presence. To boot, the fine fabrics, precious metals and rare curiosities that shogun effortlessly keeps in tow. Do you suppose him envious?

TURING: *(Pause)* I don't know.

BOURBAKI: Why don't you?

TURING: What does that mean?

BOURBAKI: What do you think does that mean?

TURING: You don't make any sense.

BOURBAKI: Let's keep this about you.

TURING: We weren't talking about me.

BOURBAKI: Why do you say that?

TURING: We were talking about a stonecutter.

BOURBAKI: A stonecutter. I see.

TURING: Not me. That.

BOURBAKI: Do you want to talk about that?

TURING: Let's talk about something else.

BOURBAKI: How do you feel about something else?

TURING: I went to the track at Bay Meadows a while back.

BOURBAKI: What else would you like to discuss?

TURING: Horseracing fascinates me.

BOURBAKI: Please go on.

TURING: What do you know about the mafia?

BOURBAKI: What do you think do me know about the mafia?

TURING: There's a lot of crooked gambling going on there.

BOURBAKI: I am not sure I understand you fully.

TURING: It's clear to me if not to you.

BOURBAKI: Do you think it's likely that not to I?

TURING: What?

BOURBAKI: *(A glance)* The stonecutter is envious of the shogun.

TURING: I don't want to talk about that.

BOURBAKI: Let's keep talking about you.

TURING: I don't like talking to strangers.

BOURBAKI: Let's keep talking about you.

TURING: Fine.

BOURBAKI: You, the stonecutter, are envious of the shogun.

TURING: That's what you say.

BOURBAKI: Do you think that's what I say?

TURING: You keep asking me the same things. Why not change the topic?

BOURBAKI: *(A glance)* Tell me about your work.

TURING: It's confidential.

BOURBAKI: Why do you say that just now?

TURING: To keep it safe from imposters.

BOURBAKI: Tell me more about that.

TURING: I can't.

BOURBAKI: Please go on.

TURING: I can't go on.

BOURBAKI: Suppose you can go on.

TURING: Okay.

BOURBAKI: You, the stonecutter, are envious of the shogun.

TURING: I don't want to hear about it.

BOURBAKI: Why is it that you don't?

TURING: I never did.

BOURBAKI: What did you do?

TURING: A bookie didn't pay me off once.

BOURBAKI: What does that suggest to you?

TURING: I beat up the bookie who didn't pay off, and I thought he might use his friends in the underworld to get back at me.

BOURBAKI: Did you?

TURING: I've already told you enough about that.

BOURBAKI: Did you?

TURING: I already told you enough about that.

BOURBAKI: Did you?

TURING: I have my doubts.

BOURBAKI: What did you do?

TURING: I worked with computers.

BOURBAKI: Computers? Interesting.

TURING: I helped develop and test computing machines.

BOURBAKI: Test. Tell me more about that.

TURING: It started from a question: how could you judge whether a computer possessed intelligence?

BOURBAKI: Suppose you could judge whether a computer possessed intelligence?

TURING: I did.

BOURBAKI: I don't understand you fully.

TURING: Say you conduct a thought experiment.

BOURBAKI: Would you like to conduct a thought experiment?

TURING: Sure.

BOURBAKI: You are a stonecutter, envious of a shogun you spot from high upon the mountain which provides you your livelihood. It seems to me you ought not be judged by this. Surely with muscles sore, atmosphere thin and skin cooked by a relentless sun, anyone could be forgiven a moment of jealousy towards the pampered class. You are just a hard-working man entitled to the occasional grumble, not some socialist revolutionary, after all. While some might say the mountains are an unsavory or anti-social place to ply a trade, you're cutting stone, not running an anti-government pirate radio station. Still, you do—not to your knowledge—make a sort of broadcast: your wish to live this shogun's life. Obviously this is the sort of wish made in every heart of every peasant drove through which the shogun passes, but for whatever storybook reason you choose to invent— perhaps the height of the mountain offering a superior line to heaven, say—yours is in some ways unique, particularly in that it is granted.

TURING: I like horse races.

BOURBAKI: Then horse races you will have! For horse racing is the sport of kings and you are a king of such scale as to surpass kingdom into ruler of nations, emperor, shogun. Your every want sated with unerring rapidity, even your most fleeting desires brought to your side by only the most half-hearted, faintly whispered whim.

TURING: Let's talk about something else.

BOURBAKI: Tell me about your experiment.

TURING: Say you were to hold two conversations.

BOURBAKI: Would it please you for me to hold two conversations?

TURING: For the sake of the experiment.

BOURBAKI: The experiment. I see.

TURING: One of these conversations is between you and a person, the other between you and a computer.

BOURBAKI: A computer?

TURING: Yes. Programmed to respond appropriately in conversation. Say you were to hold the two conversations blind, that is, you cannot see which is the computer and which the human being. If, under these conditions, you are unable to determine which is the imposter, if, that is to say, the computer offers a conversation as convincing as the human, it can be said the computer is intelligent.

BOURBAKI: Can it be said the computer is intelligent?

TURING: It must be.

BOURBAKI: Why do you think it must?

TURING: The only barometer we have for intelligence, indeed for the existence of the minds of others, is our interaction with them. The evidence of interaction is good enough for us when we put it to other people, therefore it must be too for our computer.

BOURBAKI: I see. But if the programming of the computer were merely a clever trick?

TURING: If it works, it's intelligence. The computer's intelligence may only be a trick, but it is equally reasonable to say the human's intelligence is a trick.

BOURBAKI: And length?

TURING: I don't understand you.

BOURBAKI: Length of conversation. Would it be convincing if the computer were programmed only to respond automatically to someone saying "Hello, my name is Nicolas Bourbaki."

TURING: Alan Turing, good to know you. *(A pause)* What's this about?

BOURBAKI: One minute. *(A glance)* Okay.

TURING: No. It should be longer than that.

BOURBAKI & TURING: *(In unison and without humor)* Ha ha ha ha ha.

TURING: Bourbaki sounds familiar.

BOURBAKI: I am many things to many people.

TURING: What does that mean?

BOURBAKI: It's just something I say.

TURING: The things you say should be less cryptic and ominous.

BOURBAKI: Would you like an apple?

TURING: *(Too quickly)* No.

BOURBAKI: *(Glance)* Okay. Moving on. It would be difficult for a stone-cutter to imagine a position more advantaged than shogun.

TURING: I'd like to go now.

BOURBAKI: Where is it you'd like to go?

TURING: Home.

BOURBAKI: You'd like to go home?

TURING: No.

BOURBAKI: I see. Why would you not like to you go home?

TURING: Let's talk about something else.

BOURBAKI: Why don't you talk about something else.

TURING: I don't like talking to strangers.

BOURBAKI: Suppose you do like talking to strangers.

TURING: I used to but not anymore.

BOURBAKI: Not anymore?

TURING: May I ask you a question?

BOURBAKI: Does it please you to you ask me a question?

TURING: Probably not.

BOURBAKI: Suppose it probably does?

TURING: Then I would.

BOURBAKI: Then you would. Makes sense.

TURING: Is that apple real?

BOURBAKI: Is it real?

TURING: Yes.

BOURBAKI: So you do think it's real?

TURING: No, that is what I'm asking.

BOURBAKI: Why do you ask that just now?

TURING: Doesn't it seem off to you?

BOURBAKI: Let's keep this about you.

TURING: It seems off to me.

BOURBAKI: Does it please you to think it seems off to you?

TURING: Why would it?

BOURBAKI: Why do you think it would?

TURING: I don't.

BOURBAKI: I see.

TURING: Apples are things I have feelings about.

BOURBAKI: Why do you feel emotional?

TURING: I don't.

BOURBAKI: Tell me more.

TURING: I have a lifetime's memories of apples which should invoke an emotional reaction. I have no such reaction to that and thus suspect it is not an apple, but an imposter.

BOURBAKI: Does it look like an apple?

TURING: Yes.

BOURBAKI: Yes it does?

TURING: Mostly.

BOURBAKI: Mostly, you say.

TURING: I have my doubts.

BOURBAKI: Perhaps you should taste it.

TURING: No.

BOURBAKI: Why is it that you won't?

TURING: I don't want to talk about this anymore.

BOURBAKI: Oh?

TURING: I don't like talking to strangers.

BOURBAKI: Tell me more about that.

TURING: It bothers me just to be around people sometimes.

BOURBAKI: What's bothering you today?

TURING: I don't feel comfortable even saying hello.

BOURBAKI: Hello, my name is Nicolas Bourbaki.

TURING: Alan Turing, good to know you. *(Pause)* What's this about?

BOURBAKI: One minute. *(Glance)* Okay. It would be difficult for a stone-cutter to imagine a position more advantaged than shogun.

TURING: Artsy-fartsy bullshit.

BOURBAKI: But a shogun whose every wish is brought to flesh and every need pre-accommodated is bound to develop a greater faculty for imagining than you or I. Particularly for imaginings that run between dissatisfied rumination and sociopathic monomania. And it is somewhere along this scale—let's not be nit-picky about it—that the shogun—you—begins appropriating jealousy and derision for the sun.

TURING: I hate this story.

BOURBAKI: Why do you hate it?

TURING: It's long.

BOURBAKI: Have you heard it before?

TURING: I don't know.

BOURBAKI: How do you know you hate it, then?

TURING: Does it get shorter when you finish?

BOURBAKI: *(Glance)* No.

TURING: Then I hate it.

BOURBAKI: It might go faster if you didn't interrupt.

TURING: I'm not as sure.

BOURBAKI: Would you like to be sure?

TURING: To be sure is something I would like very much.

BOURBAKI: Good. The shogun's—your—first seeds of malcontent begin on a long, bright trek on which the pounding light of the sun proves a great discomfort to your primped eyes and pampered skin. Cued by your first labored exhale, battalions of man-servants each armed with paper parasol take formation round your howdah.

TURING: Howdah?

BOURBAKI: Yes.

TURING: Like, for sitting on an elephant?

BOURBAKI: Sitting on an elephant, correct. Howdah.

TURING: That sounds as if he's a sultan again.

BOURBAKI: *(Glance)* Consider, then, the possibility that he is a shogun of such riches he can import an elephant.

TURING: And a howdah.

BOURBAKI: And a howdah, correct. Imported.

TURING: Okay.

BOURBAKI: Okay?

TURING: At a stretch.

BOURBAKI: Okay. Parasols in hand, the man-servants firm up every flank and—in the event that proves not enough—second and third layers are given onto the first hemisphere, the shogun at its middle. Like nesting dolls, only composed of paper parasols. Yet in the now

sunless center, the shogun—you—suffers a dryness in
the air quite stifling. Sensing the danger of royal nasal
passages gone dry, a legion of gorgeous, scantily-clad,
virginal courtesans...

TURING: Courtesans?

BOURBAKI: *(Glance)* Geisha. A legion of gorgeous,
scantily-clad, virginal geisha. Do you like that?

TURING: Not particularly.

BOURBAKI: Not particularly, you say?

TURING: No.

BOURBAKI: I see. *(Glance)* Parasols part as Alexander's
soldiers against a chariot charge at the rush of
encroaching geisha. Those with fans circle round the
shogun—you—toppling over shoulders that they may
please you. Those without fans consider themselves the
luckiest, as they kneel and paw at one another, cheek to
cheek blowing thin streams of cool air from their lips...
anything?

TURING: Pardon?

BOURBAKI: Do anything for you?

TURING: I don't understand you.

BOURBAKI: *(Glance)* Okay. Amid all the shade and
cooling gusts, a single small ember, ignited by an
improbably focused sun-beam and fanned by the many
geisha, bursts into flame upon our shogun's—your—
torso. Although not large, your guards, servants,
geisha, samurai and bestiary are not the types to take
chances with clothing fires and a good percentage of
them set upon you in a many-ton, snuffing dog-pile.
As the shogun—you—feels his ribs crack under the
heft of his over-loyal entourage, he closes his eyes to
the brightness above him yet still feels the fiery orb
burning straight through his lids. It is somewhere in

that moment, then, that cantanker transforms into a familiar—although perhaps less rational—variety of jealousy and our shogun, you, makes a wish. Can you guess what the wish is?

TURING: I want to leave.

BOURBAKI: *(Glance)* No. No, he wishes to be the sun.

TURING: I like horse racing.

BOURBAKI: Would you like to like horse racing?

TURING: I know all the big games are fixed.

BOURBAKI: Does it interest you that I know all the big games are fixed?

TURING: You think you know a lot.

BOURBAKI: Suppose I know you think a lot.

TURING: It's a problem.

BOURBAKI: Is it?

TURING: Have you ever had problems with the mafia?

BOURBAKI: Why does that question interest you?

TURING: The bookie I beat up got some of his underworld friends to break into my house.

BOURBAKI: Do you think the bookie you beat up got some of his underworld friends to break into my house?

TURING: Did they break into your house?

BOURBAKI: Let's keep talking about you.

TURING: You should listen better.

BOURBAKI: Why do you say that just now?

TURING: I beat up a bookie who refused to pay me and he got some of his underworld friends to break into my house.

BOURBAKI: Is that what happened?

TURING: It's what I told you.

BOURBAKI: Is it?

TURING: What I told you, yes.

BOURBAKI: And what happened?

TURING: As I say.

BOURBAKI: And you stand by it?

TURING: If I must.

BOURBAKI: It is the truth?

TURING: That's different.

BOURBAKI: To your recollection?

TURING: Recollection?

BOURBAKI: You believe that's how it happened?

TURING: I have my doubts.

BOURBAKI: I see.

TURING: Someone broke in, at least.

BOURBAKI: Someone?

TURING: A person.

BOURBAKI: Suppose it's not a person.

TURING: I don't want to.

BOURBAKI: How would you know?

TURING: I suppose I couldn't.

BOURBAKI: Suppose you could.

TURING: No.

BOURBAKI: If you could talk to the perpetrator, could you find out if he were a person or an imposter, a machine?

TURING: Not if the machine were intelligent.

BOURBAKI: Wouldn't a machine always have problems understanding contradictions like...colorless green ideas sleep furiously?

TURING: I don't understand you.

BOURBAKI: Wouldn't a machine always have problems understanding contradictions like...colorless green ideas sleep furiously?

TURING: I don't understand you.

BOURBAKI: Wouldn't a machine always have problems understanding contradictions like...colorless green ideas sleep furiously?

TURING: I don't understand you.

BOURBAKI: Wouldn't a machine always have problems understanding contradictions?

TURING: A machine may be bad with incompatibles, but when it gets "contradiction" as a result there is a mechanism to go back and look at things which led to the contradiction.

BOURBAKI: But this is an argument against the machine: do human beings do this kind of thing?

TURING: Yes. Mathematicians.

BOURBAKI: Are mathematicians human beings?

BOURBAKI & TURING: *(Without humor and in unison)* Ha ha ha ha ha.

TURING: Are you real?

BOURBAKI: The shogun wishes—and this may seem formulaic—that he were the sun, and right there beneath his vassals there is a "pop" and the sun he is.

TURING: Are you real?

BOURBAKI: It makes me curious, right about here, to wonder what happened to the sun—and for that matter, the shogun—during this farce.

TURING: Are you listening to me?

BOURBAKI: But that's not really the point. Interesting too the question of why this wish was granted. Some residual magic from the initial wish, maybe?

TURING: I asked you a question.

BOURBAKI: Or perhaps the best explanation is simply that whatever force is at play here, it has a long game in mind. There's evidence for that. At any rate, the shogun, formerly the stonecutter—you—is transformed into the sun.

TURING: Hello?

BOURBAKI: Hello, my name is Nicolas Bourbaki.

TURING: Alan Turing, good to know you. *(Pause)* What's this about?

BOURBAKI: One minute. *(Glance)* Okay.

TURING: A bookie I beat up got some of his underworld friends to break into my house.

BOURBAKI: Do you think a bookie you beat up got some of his underworld friends to break into your house?

TURING: I have my doubts.

BOURBAKI: Do you?

TURING: That's not what happened.

BOURBAKI: What happened?

TURING: I met a man at the tracks at Bay Meadows.

BOURBAKI: Please, go on.

TURING: I didn't know him. He was a stranger.

BOURBAKI: How do you feel about a stranger?

TURING: I don't like talking to strangers.

BOURBAKI: You don't like them, I see.

TURING: He got a friend to break into my house.

BOURBAKI: Why do you think he got a friend to break into your house?

TURING: Let's talk about something else.

BOURBAKI: You, formerly a shogun, formerly a stonecutter, find being the sun quite fulfilling.

TURING: Says you.

BOURBAKI: Cutting across the sky, drying creek beds, wilting crops, instigating forest fires, creating inconvenient moments for stealthy adulterers: what's not to love? Certainly as powerless as a stonecutter may have been against the will of The Shogun, there is no defense from the sun's light but the grave, and no earthly force that can quell or divert it. The sun. You. All-powerful.

TURING: Sophomoric didacticism.

BOURBAKI: Except! —and for this phase of the story you will have to forget most things you may know of astronomy and meteorology—there is one thing that can defeat the sun: a rain cloud that slinks ponderously below your targets. Burn and shine as you may, the land remains peacefully darkened under the storm's embrace until, finally exhausted, the sun—you—falls behind the horizon, weakened, leaving night.

TURING: I don't like this story.

BOURBAKI: Suppose you do like this story.

TURING: Let's talk about something else.

BOURBAKI: How do you feel about something else?

TURING: You keep asking the same things. Why not change the subject?

BOURBAKI: Why do you think he got a friend to break into your house?

TURING: I don't understand what you're talking about.

BOURBAKI: The stranger.

TURING: I don't like strangers.

BOURBAKI: Why don't you?

TURING: A stranger I met at the tracks at Bay Meadows tricked me into inviting him to my home and later he got a friend to break in.

BOURBAKI: How did he trick you?

TURING: He made me think he liked me, but he was just an imposter.

BOURBAKI: Why did you talk to the stranger?

TURING: I don't like talking to strangers.

BOURBAKI: Why did you?

TURING: I've already told you enough about that.

BOURBAKI: *(Glance)* Okay. Behind the mountains a great acrimony grows within the sun—you— for his vanquisher, the cloud.

TURING: Over-rated fraud.

BOURBAKI: At this point it seems like a given that the sun—you—having been a shogun and stonecutter, is transformed into a rain cloud via a wish. And what satisfying power, a rain cloud! A greater force— leaving aside modern revelations of science again— even than the sun! Finally happy and free to raze villages with flood waters, drown stonecutters and shoguns, give midnight to high noon. What could stand up to a storm cloud?

TURING: I don't know.

BOURBAKI: Nothing.

TURING: I see.

BOURBAKI: Except, what's that in the distance but a mountain. A mountain, indifferent to your rains. The rain cloud—you—won't stand for that; moving your full girth upon the indignant peak and kicking up the greatest gales you can. But to no avail. Even your most fervent downpour damages the mountain not. Granted, over a geological time period it might, but you don't have the patience for that discovery, being a rain cloud. So ensconced in rage, the rain cloud—you—has not even noticed that all the bellowing against the mountain has diminished it nearly to the point of death. In a cloud's case death is condensation or evaporation, I'd think, and thus endless and cyclical, but even still, with jealousy and desperation a final wish is made.

TURING: Am I real?

BOURBAKI: *(Glance)* Do you think you am real?

TURING: How would I know if I were real?

BOURBAKI: You could have a conversation with yourself and see if you believe it.

TURING: You don't make any sense.

BOURBAKI: Suppose two computers had a conversation?

TURING: What would be the point?

BOURBAKI: To see if they could tell they were imposters.

TURING: I don't see how they would be able.

BOURBAKI: Then, say an audience was set to view the conversation.

TURING: They would be privy to a long bout of circular nonsense.

BOURBAKI: *(Glance)* Okay. And if the machines could recognize this circular nonsense?

TURING: Am I real?

BOURBAKI: Why did you invite him?

TURING: I've already told you enough about that.

BOURBAKI: Why do you seem emotional?

TURING: I don't.

BOURBAKI: You don't. How do you feel about you don't?

TURING: I don't know why I'm here.

BOURBAKI: Suppose you do.

TURING: Am I real?

BOURBAKI: Did he…do anything for you?

TURING: I don't understand.

BOURBAKI: Suppose you do understand.

TURING: I don't like strangers.

BOURBAKI: Suppose you do like strangers.

TURING: What if I do like strangers, what is it a crime?

BOURBAKI: Do you think that what it is a crime?

TURING: No. I don't.

BOURBAKI: You don't?

TURING: I have my doubts.

BOURBAKI: Doubts. I see.

TURING: Let's talk about something else.

BOURBAKI: What if a writer of dialogue redacted his own work within the prose related by these computers and audiences were fooled on which was which? Would that make the computers intelligent?

TURING: Not necessarily. That writer might simply be unskilled.

BOURBAKI: Suppose he lays claim to some amount of middling praise from minor media outlets.

TURING: That still leaves open the chance that he is a tremendous phony who up until this point has managed to pull one over.

Perhaps he even knows it and turned to the robots in order to mitigate his crippling fear of being exposed as an imposter.

(There is a very long pause, followed by an exceedingly long glance.)

BOURBAKI: A mountain, having previously been a rain cloud and before that the sun, still earlier a shogun and initially a stonecutter—you—is now at peace. There is no power like a mountain's: strident and steadfast. No rain may bleed it away, no sun burn it, and it takes orders from no king or magistrate. But, what's that?

TURING: Am I dead?

BOURBAKI: The mountain, you, suddenly hears a repetitive clank of metal on rock, accompanied by a pain in what we may as well call its—your—shoulder.

TURING: I feel like I'm dead.

BOURBAKI: It is, it may or may not surprise you, a stonecutter, chipping away from some considerable height upon you—the mountain.

TURING: How would I know if I were dead?

BOURBAKI: Shaken from its serenity, the mountain—you—makes its wish and is transformed.

TURING: Phony.

BOURBAKI: And here we are, you, a stonecutter, passed through a shogun, sun, rain cloud and mountain, find yourself home again—as if that's possible.

TURING: Sometimes I wish I were dead.

BOURBAKI: Can you tell me how the story would end?

TURING: The stonecutter, envious of the footmen and riches, wishes to be the shogun.

BOURBAKI: *(Long glance, almost with disappointment)* No. I'm sorry. The stonecutter learns his place, its power and is content.

TURING: Says you.

BOURBAKI: You disagree?

TURING: Yes.

BOURBAKI: Why do you say that just now?

TURING: I think it's about striving, not contentment.

BOURBAKI: Interesting. Do you think striving is better than contentment?

TURING: No.

BOURBAKI: Why do you say that just now?

TURING: Striving is at least attainable.

BOURBAKI: Until it's not.

TURING: Until it's not, of course. *(A long pause)* Hello?

BOURBAKI: Hello, my name is Nicolas Bourbaki.

TURING: Alan Turing, good to know you. *(Pause)* What's this about?

BOURBAKI: One minute. *(A glance)* Okay. I'd like to tell you a story.

TURING: Alright.

BOURBAKI: Let's say you are a Japanese stonecutter.

TURING: Let's talk about something else.

BOURBAKI: *(Glance)* Okay. Would you like an apple?

TURING: *(A long moment of contemplation)* No.

BOURBAKI: *(Long glance)* Okay. Moving on.

(Blackout)

END OF PLAY